Advance Praise for Come Sit with Me

John W. Jenkins has captured the flavor of living in Camp Verde and serving in the Verde Valley. His book "Come Sit With Me" is an absolute delight to read. Each of his "stories" is short, concise and gives the flavor of being there and learning from each situation. I identified personally with many of the stories from "Canyon Flight," the tragic death of Carl Goswick, Dave Murdock's outsmarting the DMV because you didn't need a license to drive a farming tractor in a farming community, and finally John's telling of Tuffy Peach and the formation of Potato Lake by a source from outer space.

I count it an honor to know John not only as my pastor, but as a friend and certainly as a man of tremendous knowledge and wisdom with a shadow twice his size filled with love and compassion for those whom he encounters.

John, I trust many more will come sit with you! God Bless you and thank you for sharing your life and stories.

Charlie German, resident of Camp Verde since 1951 and
Mayor of Camp Verde

Aside from the fact that John Jenkins wrote for every newspaper in Camp Verde except the one I worked for, I must admit, he is a wonderful and insightful writer.

Put simply, his new book, *Come Sit With Me,* is a song to the place he calls home, a hymn to those whose paths he has crossed and the sanguine musing of one who clearly places a high value on living a well-examined life. It is not a long read, nor a scholarly read, but you will be a better person by the time you finish.

Steve Ayers, Recovering journalist and author of
Camp Verde (Images of America)

Come Sit With Me

John W. Jenkins

John W. Jenkins
Email: johnfocusmonk@gmail.com

ISBN:10:1986542556
ISBN-13: 978986542556

DEDICATION

I dedicate *Come Sit With Me* to the memory
of my dear wife and faithful friend
Doris Jenkins
and her sixty years of faithful love and support.

CONTENTS

Introduction   i

My Big Five-O   1

Doris and the Slots   6

The Single Gift   9

Daddy   11

Little Girl Lost   12

The Fawn   14

Verde West Quail   18

Birds and Squirrels   20

A Rabbit Named Harry   23

Weed Eaters   25

Musings of a Beekeeping Minister   28

My Money Tree   34

Born Wild   37

The Rattle Snake   40

Scott and Linda Dieringer   42

Cowboys, Horses, Cattle, & Lions   45

Dave Murdoch   48

Mr. Gardner's Kellogg Job   52

Rena Frew   54

Carl Goswick   56

Hospital Housekeeping   60

Naturally   63

Send in The Clowns   67

Itch and Scratch   69

Nuclear Roulette   72

Monticello   76

America   78

The Library   80

On the Road with Kids   83

Mexican Black Vultures   85

Over Mingus Mountain   86

Blueberry Hill   89

Empty Places and Spaces   92

What If   95

Senior Christians   98

The Marriage Candle   100

Old Catholic Churches   103

Alan Sees God   105

Heaven and Hell   109

Our Robot   110

The Mysterious   113

The Current Beneath   116

Dante's View   119

High Desert Gold 123

Macho Tom 125

Dog Days 128

Dancing With Dogs 130

Canyon Flight 134

Up, Up and Away 137

The Scout Master 140

Visitors 145

January Rain 148

El Toro Storms 150

Monarch Ponderosa 151

The Rainbow 153

Art 155

The Dark of December 159

Knoll Lake 161

Chevelon Canyon 163

Five Pounds 167

Potato Lake 170

Living Water 172

Good Medicine 175

Roosevelt Lake 177

Acknowledgements 181

About the Author 183

Introduction

"The earth's a stage which God and nature do with actors fill." Thomas Heywood

I don't write for profit though profit is important. I don't write for readership and popularity though I receive both with gratitude. I write because I must write.

We are all passengers on planet earth, orbiting our sun in the Milky Way, in a universe of galaxies. Furthermore, we are all on personal journeys and each have stories of our journey.

Our birth-package includes the gifts of freedom and imagination, along with that pesky cause and effect clause. At times my stories may have the catalyst of humor, and taboos for effect, offensive to some, insightful to others.

In this book I share my stories and the stories of others. Come sit with me. Some of my stories originated decades ago in my home town newspaper, *The Verde View* and later *The Journal* (Camp Verde, Arizona). Other stories are archived in my journals and diaries. I vividly remember most.

A few stories are of my Southwest travel. Others are of people, animals, artful beauty, religious and philosophical themes, sometimes tragedies, but most are of happy and humorous times and places—like our visit to a Las Vegas casino where Doris lost nickels in a slot machine.

Always, good drama needs protagonists and antagonists with their many shades of gray actors. Ah, the bittersweet gifts of free will and imagination. We are all actors on the stage of life. And like all good drama, our lives may suddenly turn on a dime and lift us into exciting insights, or move us into scary unknowns. Old mornings pass away, new mornings come again and again, in which we write new chapters in our books of transformations.

I believe one story helps set the mood of this book: Years ago, Doris and I visited the Lady Bird Johnson Redwood Forest in northern California and we walked the winding trail among ancient redwood trees. I photographed a bench for two. There we sat quietly and rested for a time and listened to the slight breeze whisper in the tops of redwoods. It was an ancient whisper, more ancient than the trees. Resting there, the seeds of my book came to me.

As we sat under these giant trees, I thought of their towering life, begun as wispy wands with meager needle-leaves that could easily be counted. They had been given a gift of life and a small shaft of light to follow to open sky. And they did.

I invite you to come and sit with me. Together we shall wait for the patient One to come and whisper soft and slow in silent voice that only the mind can hear and the heart can know. Perhaps it will show us a shaft of light to follow.

I appreciate Albert Einstein's thought: "The most beautiful emotion we can experience is the mysterious. It is the source of all true art and science. He to whom this emotion is a stranger, who can no longer pause to wonder and become rapt in awe is as good as dead. His eyes are closed. To know that what is impenetrable to us really exists, manifesting itself to us as the highest wisdom and the most radiant beauty, which our dull faculties can comprehend only in their most primitive forms. This knowledge, this feeling is at the centre of all true religiousness. In this sense, and in this sense only, I belong to the ranks of devoutly religious men."

A rainbow arched and touched the valley last week; it lightly touched the ground with its Christmas candy colors. The rainbow was a child of rain and sunshine, phenomena born of water and light. I watched it slowly drift through a field of mesquite and when the band of colors passed through a single tree, it blazed with cold fire. I watched until it passed beyond a ridge—out of sight.

The necessary discipline of science in its soft war with ignorance and superstition is concerned primarily with water, light and refraction, which leaves little room for divine promise or spiritual meaning.

Consequently the mystical meaning of rainbows is left to poets, children, artists, and pious folks who see God hiding in plain sight, who see wonder in ordinary things.

I followed my yellow brick road and found my home again. It's in the heart. Now, come and sit with me and I will share my stories.

John W. Jenkins
March, 2018
Camp Verde, Arizona

My Big Five-O

The Big Five-O is a prestigious trophy given to anyone who has survived fifty years in the twentieth century—no small task.

This week I received this award when I turned the half-century corner of my life. Though my birth certificate—my Alpha—secretly honors the event, my calendar honors my personal journey. White hair, a beginning second chin, and faint crow's feet around my eyes mark the occasion.

I now know fifty years of sand time have trickled through the narrow neck of my hourglass of changes into its bell-bottom; and I now know fifty years of my allotted time have become my yesterdays. I like the hour glass metaphor.

Fortunately, I have not lost my youthful love of life. Furthermore, nothing escapes my curiosity; nothing escapes my interest in theology and the sciences.

I have survived bad choices, bad company, and critics; plus near fatal diseases, crime, the Cold War, accidents, all degrees of weather, environmental pollutants, not without some psychical and physical scars and damage —I'm sure.

I've accumulated by wind enough low level radio activity from nuclear bomb testing, foreign and domestic, during the Cold War to wiggle the needle of a Geiger counter.

Furthermore, I've consumed enough DDT pesticide to kill bugs and bees and ruin eggs of birds.

I know I have enough cancer-causing chemicals embedded in my bones, enough lead from old-time lead gasoline and crib paint, and enough mercury from eating fish and drinking water to frostbite my DNA.

I have absorbed enough pollutants in our atmosphere and poisons in my food, no thanks to the nuclear, chemical and energy industries. It's a wonder I'm not an invalid drooling in my oatmeal. I thank my body for its amazing ability to renew itself every seven years—so I'm told.

Once more, you would presume that I'm no longer a threat to society—not so. I'm still measured and scanned by ceiling cameras in banks, grocery stores, schools, and public places—especially air terminals and courthouses.

Furthermore, I'm constantly being measured by society, government, and insurance actuaries, which predicts my probable life span based on my age, geo-location, income and gender.

My doctor says I'll live to be a hundred. Humm, I wonder? I told him that it would be fine if I'm still alive and didn't take my last ten years to die. He laughed. Not wanting to appear ungrateful, I laughed, too. No one knows when their time is up, of course. Neither doctors nor anyone else are on that policy-making level.

I'm thankful for my ancestors' DNA package and for medical science for conquering diseases that once crippled and killed them long before their fifties. I'm grateful for my good health, free of pain and disabilities.

I honor my life's contract by helping nature keep me alive and healthy. I eat my weeds and seeds, grains and nuts, berries, veggies and fruit, and meat cooked past red— no *E. coli*. I keep my weight within the blue section of weight charts. Furthermore, I exercise and nourish my spiritual and mental health through meditation. Whew! Keeping alive is not easy. Some people would rather die and be done with it.

My Big Five-O is middle-age-adolescence; no one listens and no one cares. When I mention my fifty years in the presence of older folks, I usually get a blank stare or a sly smile that conceals some hidden secret that I'm too young to understand. More annoying, though, some laugh and change the subject.

When I mention my fifty years in the presence of young adults they merely look past me at some distant cemetery tomb stone with engraved dates, or envision my slow slide into senility. Some out of politeness share stories of uncles and grandparents who successfully hobbled through their sixties into their seventies before they became burdens to their children. These success stories only make my middle-age-adolescence more painful. Sometimes I wish I hadn't made my hole-in-one.

I've discovered that I'm out of my known past and not quite in my unknown future. At fifty I'm either too old or too young for most people around me.

Being fifty is an awkward age. When you are fifty, young ladies say that you remind them of their grandfathers, and young men avoid you out of fear of witnessing a heart attack.

You know you are fifty when you finish in the bottom third of your community's Jog-a-thon. You know you are fifty when a lively euthanasia discussion abruptly stops when the group sees you coming.

Fifty is old enough to join the local senior citizen's group and receive a discount on meal—embarrassing for some.

Fifty has too many embarrassing moments. For instance, after you've finally found an opening in the conversation and have insinuated your half-dozen grandchildren into public domain—before you can draw out photos—someone older beats you to the draw with photos of their great-grandchildren. High Noon déjà vu. Thanks for trying.

There ought to be a Big Five-O halfway house for folks like us; sheltered places where we can lay back, mellow out, and adjust to our changed social status. I met a person the other day who will soon be fifty and I thought of him as a long, lost brother. Women don't admit it.

In spite of my complaints, I like being fifty now that I've learned the ground rules. Fifty is a good time to have a wife near the Big Five-O, and it's a good time to drop some of those heavy responsibilities into the lap of my replacement generation.

Fifty is a good time to take inventory of my body and to make necessary adjustments before slipping into the sixties and seventies—and beyond, if the Good Lord permits. It's a great time to make peace with ambition and expectation, and throttle back that youth-driven engine that relentlessly moved me to where I now stand.

The way I see it, my Big Five-O is a golfer's hole-in-one, normally a once in a lifetime celebration, a gold watch occasion, retirement the next morning. You got this one, but getting another is unlikely. But like a golfer who never gives up, I plan to celebrate my Big **100** hole-in-one, or is it a hole in two?

Now that I've got The Big Five-O out of the way, I seriously think Dylan Thomas' insightful poem, "Do not Go Gentle into That Good Night." I plan not to go gently into my next Five-O, maybe years beyond.

This I know: my final inventory is coming and I will need my Creator's love and grace for that. Maybe I'll get points for joyful effort. Then I will accelerate out of time and space into my big Omega.

* * *

At the time of book's writing in 2018, I am eighty-eight and in good health, thanks to my Creator, ancestors and my own desire to avoid pain and shame and be fully alive. Though not a golfer, I know some of the rules. After many golf balls lobbed into sand traps, woods, lily ponds, and tee to greens, I may make my second hole-in-one. We'll see.

A version of "My Big Five-O" was published in the *Verde View*, April 10-16, 1980.

Doris and the Slots

"God has a great sense of humor; he's just working with a slow audience." Garrison Keillor

The day Doris and I visited a Nevada casino and tasted the bitter-sweet fruit of risk and chance may not have been much in the gambling, whoops, gaming business.

But for us it has become a gold mine of humorous trivia. If one is to have a vice, it should be humorous, legal, and trivial.

Everyone should taste at least once the sweet fruit of sudden wealth that bypasses honest labor, coupled with sudden poverty, if only to escape self-righteousness and prudery. Therefore, I say, listen to Lady Luck for she has much to teach us about gain and loss, illusion and reality, greed and responsibility. It's good to know when to hold and when to fold before betting your house and retirement at a blackjack table or slot.

Thankfully, Doris' brief venture into the gaming business is the moral equivalent of that extra piece of pie and "darn" in a flash of anger. Also, her sudden impulse to risk hard cash for quick profit merely proves her common bond with the rest of us, which is wonderfully humbling.

Her slight slip into gaming is a sensitive subject needing public confession, if only to scratch an itchy conscience and restore original grace. Even so, in spite of absolution, there's no escaping consequences. To this day Doris carries the imprint of her indiscretion. For instance: "you bet" and "the odds are against it" have noticeably popped up in her everyday conversation. Also, when she deposits coins in parking meters, she lingers a little too long for my comfort. I suspect she's hoping for a trio of cherries or oranges to roll-up in the little window. I'm concerned that after that one-time-taste of risk and chance, she will ever after be looking for easy pay offs. Thankfully, she has me to help her stay on the straight and narrow.

It all started while we were on vacation routed through Las Vegas, called Sin City by some; I don't. Some say and truly believe, "What's done in Las Vegas stays in Las Vegas," which denies embedded consequences.

As the world well knows, this Neon Strip that never sleeps is the gaming capital of our country, and gaming here is legalized, supervised, monitored, and finally taxed by the sovereign state of Nevada. The tax money pays for the highways of Nevada. Anyone who has ever driven Highway 50, the loneliest highway in the country, will appreciate the enormous benefit of the gaming tax.

Back to Doris: Her gaming interest is mostly my fault. For you see, we stopped at one of the casinos for a quick lunch before venturing on to Scotty's Castle and Death Valley, Doris' favorite vacation place.

To shorten the story, the coffee shop was closed but the gaming hall wasn't. We wandered among the poker tables and slots. Security gave us the once-over, smiled knowingly, and left us alone. The action was early morning, slow and cautious, but still green blackjack tables and idle slots cast their spells of quick wins and easy money. Who knows, we thought, maybe Lady Luck would smile on us, fix the game, and make us rich. That's when we decided to court the lady.

In the spirit of high hopes, Doris dug in her purse and came up with five nickels and seeded a slot. The sound was metallic, impersonal, and cold as cash. The lever rasped, gears meshed and whirred, fruit spun and stopped. No three of-a kind, too much variety. Silence! Nothing came out the bottom.

A customer needs to win. The house needs to stay in business through math in favor of the house (60-40?) and the illusion that Lady Luck and God favors special gamers. I know special people who win more than they lose. So they say.

Hard but true: everyone with the I.Q. of a popcorn popper knows that the Lady is married to the house. However, for the benefit of her business, the Lady is a tramp and will flirt and kiss with winnings now and then. She coyly flirted with us, but no kisses.

If we expected a kiss from The Lady, one nickel wouldn't get it. She's not cheap. To get her attention we had to be big spenders; so Doris did. She reached in her purse for more nickels and fed the slot again. She pulled the handle five more times (years before the electronic machines). More metal noise, but no return on her investment. The pretty lady remained aloof. She wanted more money. Unwilling to pay for her attention, we left her standing at the slot. Walking away, I thought: we helped Nevada pay for highways and we stood up Lady Luck.

Written in 2005.

The Single Gift

A single gift demands attention, too many hinder. A Japanese tradition emphasizes the power of singularity.

A single flower in a vase on a table in the middle of an empty room holds the attention. There's no sorting it out from among distractions. Therefore, absolute attention is focused on this single object. Nothing dulls the senses or scatters thought. No ribbons, no gilding the lily, just flower truth, flower power.

My problem was that Doris could have had what she wanted any day by shopping; however, she had no desire for lots of things. She lived simply and needed little. She was happy without abundance.

Long ago, in distant memory now, I looked for that single Christmas gift that carried the meaning of my love for Doris, my wife. It had to be something special for someone special.

Hopefully, it would be a gift that lifted her spirit and inspired her thoughts. When I found it and gave it, it would be a single gift that blessed twice.

A few days before Christmas we strolled through a shopping mall and stopped at a gift shop. She paused before a Cabbage Patch doll. Those dolls were hot items back then. I knew why she paused and looked them over. Their baby-soft vinyl faces, cute belly buttons, and dimpled knees and elbows brought back memories of her babies, perhaps her childhood dolls, all safely tucked in soft memories.

This doll came with an authentic birth certificate, adoption papers, and the promise of a greeting card on its first birthday. The birthday was the day sold.

That Christmas, this doll had captured the hearts of little girls and little girls in a mother's heart— fathers' too.

I read about a father who flew to England just to buy his little girl the doll. Flying to England, buying a doll, and then flying home added an extra layer of value to the doll.

One may question the wisdom of paying a sack of money for a store-bought doll when someone in the family could have made a cute rag doll, if such a person exists anymore. Once grandmothers and aunts made rag dolls for their little girls; maybe some do now, none that I know.

After Doris left the store, I secretly bought the Cabbage Patch Doll, along with its certificate, and asked the clerk to gift wrap it. I gave it to Doris Christmas morning. Her eyes misted, her heart sang, and she was alone in the room with her single gift, a mother with her baby, a little girl again.

A version of "The Single Gift" was published in the *Verde View*, December 21, 1983.

Daddy

I watched a young father and his little girl walk across the parking lot of McDonalds to where I sat inside.

They reminded me of the ballad: "Daddy Don't You Walk So Fast." This daddy wasn't walking too fast. It was she who was dancing circles around her towering father. He was serious, deliberate and businesslike while she danced safely in his presence. She adored him. She couldn't keep her eyes off him. She was alone with her daddy and that was just about the biggest and brightest thing that could ever happen. He was in work shirt and Levis; she wore a plain little girl's dress, but in her eyes, he was Prince Charming and she was his Cinderella.

I looked for signs of a father's love and found them. He was too serious as young fathers often are, too strong as new fathers seem to be, but his fatherhood was patient and gentle.

He moved as a man moves when he is with his daughter in public. He moved as a good man moves from fatherhood into daddy-hood. Although he was deliberate and heavy with responsibilities, he was very patient, allowing his little girl the freedom of her innocence. He gently listened to her excited chatter. After burgers and French fries together, they moved to their pickup truck where he opened the door and lifted her in.

Written in 2005.

Little Girl Lost

Up highway 260, east of Camp Verde, Arizona, a hard right up the narrow Fossil Creek Road ends at Strawberry, Arizona. On the way, near eye-blink Childs, a narrow dirt road angles down rolling hills to the decommissioned Child's Power Plant along the Verde River.

The power plant's turbines once churned electricity for mining camps, the city of Prescott and Verde Valley communities, and then joined the APS grid. Though the turbines no longer turn, the plant's buildings and campground remain at this writing. With permission or not, visitors keep coming to enjoy the picnic grounds, to relax, fish, and have access to the Verde Hot Springs just across the river.

Power plant management once maintained a lawn and provided trash containers and picnic tables for the public. An anchored hand-pulled cable seat was provided for people who visited the hot springs. Since this isolated hot springs was screened by willows and mesquites—nudity happened.

Not all people respected this unsupervised campground; vandals trashed facilities, others left trash behind. Regrettably, people in a hurry to be somewhere else left things behind and had traveled too far to return for them. A few lost valuables were found by others, or never found at all.

Good people still come and go, but not so many now. Sometimes wild parties continue through the nights, with hard drinking and drugs. A few come who must never, ever find a little lost girl.

Now begins my story of a little girl lost. My friend John and his friend Sidney visited Child's power plant camp ground in 2003 and found a little girl of three, maybe four, sitting alone at a picnic table. No one else was around. John went over to talk to her. She was scared, dirty, hungry, and thirsty. John asked her where her daddy was. She said, "I have no daddy." He then asked the girl where her mommy was. She said, "I have no mommy." John then led her to where Sid waited. They gave her a cookie and some water.

Leaving the little girl with Sid, John drove back to Camp Verde and told the Marshal that they had found a little girl alone in the Child's Power Plant campground and that Sid was watching over her. The Marshal and John drove back to the campground and the Marshal took the little girl to Camp Verde.

I asked John if the Marshal had found her parents. He didn't know.

Two good men found and protected an abandoned and scared little girl in a remote Arizona campground. Hopefully, prayerfully, this little girl found a decent home and loving parents.

John said he and Sidney looked for her story in local newspapers. Nothing had been published. Maybe the Marshal found her parents, maybe not. Most likely, she was transferred to the county's child protection agency.

Life has many twists and turns. This twist turned out well.

Written in 2003.

The Fawn

"A hawk sees the pine needle fall, a bear smells the falling pine needle, and a deer hears the drop of a pine needle in a forest." A Native Alaskan proverb

I lay quietly beside my mother and felt the warm morning sun filter through the ponderosa pine canopy and smelled the pungent forest floor, along with drifting scents of animal life.

This first hour of morning was alive with faint sounds of small animals going about their business of living. My mother listened for the slightest sound—every sound. Later black gnats swarmed in the shadows and tormented my ears and eyes.

I vaguely remember: soon after my mother gave me a bath, and as soon as I could stand on wobbly legs braced at awkward angles, each step more of a stumble than a step, she led me away from my birthplace to a shadowed shelter of ferns and sumac. Within this tangle of ferns and pine branches I was safe.

My birth scent had drifted in currents and eddies, sending the message of new-born fawn to every predator. There, I easily folded into my hiding place. There, my camouflaged coat perfectly blended with shadows and half-lights. If I remained still, I was invisible to predators. Furthermore, my new body was scentless. Although I had been in the world only a few hours, I knew to lie soundless and motionless.

I had to distrust every animal when my mother left to feed and drink. Although I had been in the world only a few hours, I knew what was expected of me when my mother was away.

If I had been discovered by a predator my mother could have inflicted terrible punishment with her sharp hooves on most small predators that threatened me, but she had no chance of saving me from a bear or mountain lion, and little chance against a pair of coyotes.

Suddenly my mother caught coyote scent and immediately searched the interspacing of the forest for her ancient enemy. Then she quickly slipped away some distance, circled to leave a decoy trail and waited. She knew that she could easily out-distance the coyote and even escape a mountain lion if she didn't panic.

A season ago, she watched a mountain lion ambush and kill her brother. The lion had launched its attack with a terrifying squall that panicked her brother. He tried to run, but his legs only moved in short, trembling steps. Such was the power of fear. She had learned the lesson of panic and was now using deception to protect her helpless fawn.

While waiting for the coyote, she thought of her first fawn. Then, she was a nervous young mother ill prepared for the pair of coyotes that had come for that fawn. Before they had discovered her fawn, she had dashed to its defense too soon, revealing its hiding place. She repeatedly struck the male coyote with her sharp front hooves—fur flew. He had paid a high price for threatening her fawn; however, her desperate defense was in vain, for though she had driven the male coyote off, his mate had slipped in and killed her fawn. She guarded her dead fawn for the rest of the day and into the night. Then she walked away from its lifeless body. The coyotes watched her leave and came back to eat.

This time she would not make that mistake. She waited in the shadows and watched the coyote search for me in ever smaller circles. I felt its coming. I froze, not even a blink or twitch of an ear, fearing the slightest movement would draw its attention. It came within a few feet of where I lay, bringing with it the foul stink of carrion. It yapped now and then to panic me into getting up and trying to run. I fought against my fear and won. Then it wandered away and was gone.

My mother waited, and then followed the coyote's scent to where it led into a deep canyon. Confident that he had lost interest and had not circled back, she circled my hiding place several times before she returned to me. We had to move immediately for he might return and catch us unprepared.

My first days were filled with danger and beauty, which set the pace of my life until it ran its natural course.

My mother told me that I must learn to escape coyotes and mountain lions. But eventually I would meet the two-legged ones with their bows and fire sticks and learn how to escape them. It was easy to know their coming for they were noisy and clumsy in the forest and smelled of grease and smoke. Their scents filled the forest. If I ran and hid immediately, I would be safe.

Then my mother said that the two-legged ones were very slow, with neither fang nor claw; therefore, without their bows and fire sticks, they were harmless. My mother also said that long distance in the open was no protection from the new hunters, for they could easily see me through their binoculars and scopes and kill at a great distance. The good ones aimed well and killed cleanly, and like a mountain lion they ate their kill. But the careless ones, full of trigger-itch, aimed poorly and often wounded us. Once more, these had neither the skill nor the desire to follow our blood trails into our hiding places.

I asked, "Why do the two-legged ones hunt us?" My mother answered, "The good hunters are living creatures too and know their place in Nature. Furthermore, these wise ones know that they are predators like wolves and lions. More importantly for us, many of the two-legged ones are spiritual beings who are awake and understand the meaning and purpose of all creatures and see the big picture of Creation. Because they know wilderness in a different way, they make good hunting laws that respect our rightful place in the animal kingdom. After they kill us, these good ones often bow their heads and apologize for taking our lives and thank the Great Spirit for the venison meat that will nourish them and their families.

"Unfortunately, other two-legged ones, those who are sleepwalking in their dreams, only value the sport of hunting and collecting our antlers."

What my mother told me hurt my ears and made me sad. Then a butterfly landed nearby. Good thoughts returned.

Verde West Quail

We are namers and counters by culture and nature. I'm told it's embedded in our genes. Those who know say that we are born knowing how to compare, compile, test, and judge.

I wonder. This I know: It's refreshing to take a break from counting and enjoy something that doesn't need my counting or judgment.

Doris and I have about 70 trees, some Arizona cypress, some fruit, and some nut. Whoops! There I go counting again. I'm amazed at how many trees we've managed to crowd into this acre, and how many quail coveys have made their night homes in our cypress.

One particular covey, the Verde West Quail, come to our trees in the evening running on a blur of tiny legs. Then from a mesquite field and across a dirt road, they fly in a whir of stubby wings up into the shadowed safety of a cypress tree. It's in the front yard. They settle and murmur among themselves like a brook singing down a mountain.

A friend once asked me how many quail were in the Verde West Covey. I hadn't counted them, I answered. Maybe a dozen or so, I opined, coming perilously close to losing them in my counting. No reason to count, for hawks, roadrunners, cats, and hunters keep changing their numbers, I added.

Sometimes in the night when counting, naming and measuring haunt the hours, I walk under the cypress for quail-therapy. Shining a light up into the cypress where they perch, I listen to their talk. I need the Verde Quail's uncounted mystery.

A time before this time, the Verde Quail were my teachers. They taught me how not to count.

A version of "Verde West Quail" was published in the *Verde View,* January 10, 1980.

Birds and Squirrels

Standing still in this paradise side of early morning, looking from my kitchen window, I watch birds feeding—a squirrel, too.

Out of the shadows of an Arizona Cypress tree, small birds swoop in low and fast landing on our bird feeders, scattering seeds in gusts of tiny wings. Then, in eye-blinks of time they shell sunflower and flax seeds with polished practice. Just arm's length from where I watch, humming birds dart, argue, hover and sip sugar syrup from their feeder. It's their feeder, not mine.

These birds neither sow nor reap, though they do pass hard seeds in wild sowing. They do not build barns, though they do build nests. Nor do they have needs beyond their wits, wings, and rearing the next generation. Of courses, some migrate when seasons compel. They live according to their needs in their niches of nature.

A hawk circles and the birds vanish into the shadows of the cypress, their tree of life. It's a good hawk, just doing a hawk's business of keeping birds strong, alert, and flying. Furthermore, the hawk promises each bird it need not be troubled by money, politics, religion, nor stocks and bonds, retirement plans, and heath care issues. There is no assistance care for birds, for they live a life that human time forgot. These birds live in moments, not days, months, nor years. Consequently, they are forever young and suffer no long good-byes. In return for its service, the hawk gets to eat the slow and witless for lunch. God feeds hawks, too.

Just to the left from where I look, I see this cypress tree I had planted when it was but a slender wand with a moist bulb for a root. This old cypress flourishes in its day, my day too. This monument to slow-growth life is now home for sparrows and hummingbirds. It teaches me that life is precious and worth living.

Where will this cypress life go when it's time for it to go? In seedlings, in the winds, in memories, in another dimension, I do not know — for sure. Will it be young again? Or will it cease to be. I hope it's in my tomorrows.

Now to a squirrel: I smile as I watch our resident squirrel stop and start, pause and dash across our lawn, then slip into the shadow of our truck or car. The hawk keeps him running in the sunshine and hiding in the shadows. Not to worry, for this squirrel is fast and smart. He has learned to live with people, hawks, cats, and cars and he's too smart to move an eye from road and sky. However, just in case the squirrel forgets, the hawk circles back, watching, ready for the smallest mistake.

Slipping in and out of shadows, our resident squirrel forages for breakfast among last fall's locust seeds (St John's-Bread), and wintered pecans. To help the squirrel, though he doesn't need my help, I sometimes toss a handful of nuts into the shadow of a tree, which eventually turn up as shells under the hood of my Nissan pickup. As long as my furry friend doesn't chew its wiring, I'll let him stay; however, if he gets a taste for insulation, I'll live trap him and transport him miles away to West Clear Creek, where I'll turn him loose, toss him a handful of pecans, and drive off. Banished to this new environment, he will need to invent a new survival game. By wits and stealth, I'm sure he'll survive, and perhaps find a mate and add his genes to the West Clear Creek squirrel gang. That is, if he keeps one eye on the ground and the other on the sky.

If the Father of birds, squirrels, and hawks gives his natural children according to their needs and as they serve according to their natures, how much more will our Father give to us according to our needs as we serve according to our needs and natures. God comes in many different forms — I believe.

P.S. I discovered that this pesky squirrel had begun to eat my pickup's insulation. I caught him in my live animal trap and introduced him to his promised land.

Written in 2016.

A Rabbit Named Harry

What does this rabbit know? What do we know about a white rabbit running loose at our place, just as free as his brown cousins in the wild?

Evidently someone dumped him in our neighborhood, and this rabbit decided to make his last stand at our place. A rabbit has a tough time in this world. Rabbits, wild or tame, are about as vulnerable as any creature can be. It can be even tougher if it's stupid.

I'm surprised he has survived as long as he has.

A domesticated hutch-bred rabbit has all its survival instincts modified to serve our needs. Outside their cages they are as helpless against predators as sheep among wolves. Too trusting, to slow, too soft, too weak, they are easy prey for any creature hungry for rabbit lunch.

When I first saw this white rabbit in our front yard trustingly eating grass, I was sure it wouldn't last the night. I was wrong. Out of respect, I named him Harry.

Harry has been here for about six months now. We don't claim him, nor does he want to be claimed. No one else does either. Fortunately for him, though, we have given him asylum and as long as he stays on our property he is allowed to eat what he wants. However, if he leaves he's on his own. We don't try to save him from his folly of raiding neighborhood gardens; amazingly, he hasn't been shot, stoned, or clubbed to death by angry gardeners, or fallen prey to coyote, hawk, or a hungry dog. Obviously, Harry is one smart rabbit living a charmed life.

Harry has taken up with our resident barn cat, Snowball. They're both half-wild, he's a buck rabbit and she's a female cat. They're both white; he is heavy; she is slim. However, these are minor differences compared to being members of incompatible species. The cat is a predator, a carnivore, while Harry is an herbivore, a prey animal. Yet they are close friends. They play, eat, and sleep together. Harry has learned to eat a little cat food now and then, which makes Harry a very compatible rabbit.

Yesterday I noticed that Harry had an injured eye. He sat very still in the shadows of the barn as if trying to understand his new challenge. Had he injured it in a fight with Snowball's friends? These other cats are scandalized by Harry's friendship with one of their own. Did he lose his eye to a BB or pellet gun? Whatever caused Harry's injury, it threatened his survival in his world of angry people and jealous toms. Just now, I hear Snowball calling for him. She is looking in all their familiar places.

Harry is just a loose rabbit and Snowball is just a common cat, but that's how we see them, not how it is. How can we know anything about how they feel about each other? We are only human.

Written in 1986.

Weed Eaters

We have three weed eaters, not the kind that buzz and fuss around the edges of sidewalks, buildings, and bushes, but the four-legged kind called goats.

We've had them long before the gas and electric jobs. They're always wound up and running, no gas or batteries, just teeth and appetite. Their teeth are more efficient than whirling monofilament fish line.

Weedies is the breakfast food of these champions, and whatever they chew and consume is finally pelletized.

My weed eaters are fat-bellied nanny goats who gently jostle each other throughout the day, thereby keeping their politics simple, free, and efficient, not the human kind. They reduce social friction by frequent head butts, fast walks to brush and weeds deliveries, saunters to shady places, and races for who gets firsts at the drinking pail. Because of gentle jostling, each goat knows who she is, what she is supposed to do, and where she belongs in the goat hierarchy.

Each morning I bribe them with oats, then Doris or I milk them, and then make sure they have alfalfa hay, weeds, and brush to munch during the day. If not, they will search the fence line, find an opening too small for even a rabbit, ream it bigger, and escape, then do goaty mayhem among our fruit trees.

They are so efficient and indiscriminate, we must keep them firmly confined within strong fences, or they will eat all our green, dead, and growing things. For if one of these goats gets loose, she will head for the prettiest rose bush, the most delicate fruit tree, and finish up with a dessert in the vegetable garden. Only then she will head for the weeds, briars, and prickly things.

Ecologists and historians tell us that uncontrolled goats multiply energetically and have been responsible for more wasteland than any other animal. They are capable of destroying a forest by first eating young trees and then debarking mature ones. Of course, left free to roam without human control and protection, Mother Nature will step in and save the world with one of her best population control tools: predators. They will chase goats onto mountain tops and keep them there.

Though goat usefulness has diminished since the industrial revolution, somewhere in the world today an indigenous tribe still depends on goats for food, clothing, and tents; and for this reason indigenous folks can enjoy free time lacking in modern cultures. Of course, once a person has suffered the good and evil fruits of the modern world, it's too difficult to go back to goaty-simplicity and have all that leisure time on their hands.

I lived in and now remember that drop out, tune in time, the summer of love in 1969, now a mere hiccup in world history. But it was a hiccup heard around the world.

Some tried communal simplicity in their revolt against the Establishment and the Man, but after their back to nature passion cooled into itchy boredom and sweaty discontent they morphed into organic farms and whole foods and environmental issues. Others joined the Culture War between the far left Progressives and the far-right Traditionalists. The far-left warriors fought with political correctness, identity politics, administrative and judicial edicts backed by noisy street protests. A radical fringe robbed banks and bombed building. Tradition warriors fought with law and order, established institutions, patriotism, time-honored ethics and proven morality. Tradition lost? Time will tell.

Back to goats: Recently Prescott National Forest management experimented with leased goats to clean the forest of fire-kindling brush and weeds. Hopefully, this experiment will become a continuing management tool.

It's comforting to know that goats are our safety nets ready to catch us if we manage to nuke ourselves into wasteland. Heaven forbid. With a few nannies and a billy, and with the common sense of a goat, along with a desire to live, we could survive. You can't say this about a Mercedes Benz parked in a driveway.

Written in 1979.

Musings of a Beekeeping Minister

Although I am still a beekeeper, I haven't kept bees since 1989. I am a beekeeper without bees. My bees now live in my memory.

Through the centuries people believed beekeeping or bee charming was a gift given to people who were gentle of heart and slow to anger. These people talked to bees, listened to their songs and understood their moods. Stoically, they accepted stings. You can't keep bees if you don't respect them and control emotions. Swatting bees only angers them. This I know: nervous, fearful, impatient, distrustful, and angry people do not keep bees for long.

I once placed half a dozen hives at a ranch at the top of Copper Canyon in Arizona. I was certain that these hives were a safe distance from the ranch house, horses and cattle. Furthermore, I believed my bees would fill a few supers with mesquite and cat claw honey and I would give a gallon or two to the rancher.

One day I attended my hives when it was cool and the bees were restless, but manageable. In full protection near an open hive, I was examining a frame of brood, and had set aside a frame of honey, when suddenly I felt a presence behind me. I turned and saw a bikini clad woman standing close. This sudden sight of so much bare skin was so out of context that at first it didn't seem real.

Obviously, she didn't know my bees would soon send guard bees and if she swatted them, they would sting. Since the odor of bee venom draws bees, this was not a good place for her to be. I firmly advised her to slowly back away and slowly go.

She did! Turns out she was a visitor from California. She had a bee encounter to remember.

Once, hoping to harvest sweet clover honey, I placed several hives in a meadow on the Apache Maid Ranch. Always when I've been invited to place hives, I promised to remove them immediately if they become a problem. One afternoon I received a phone call from the ranch informing me that cattle or horses had knocked over my hives. I rushed up to the ranch. The day was overcast, raining and cool. The bees were wet, cold and angry. Although I knew I needed a veil, gloves, and suit, I forgot my boots and duct tape to wrap my pant legs over said boots.

The bees found my ankles and zeroed in. I couldn't stop. I quickly righted the hives, got into my pickup, then scraped stingers out with my finger nails. Although I am able to receive multiple stings with little or no swelling, it still hurts. Baking soda helps.

History: In the days of horses and buggies, before gentle bees were bred, bees caused serious problems for horses and communities. Bees and horses didn't get along. Probably, their sweat, scent, and actions angered bees. Of course if bees stung a buggy horse, it could panic and run. And if a horse was corralled and couldn't get into a barn, bees could sting it to death. Stung horses could be saved with bed sheets soaked in baking soda.

Interestingly, cattle and bees get along better. A cow may suffer multiply stings and not get excited or maybe the cow's odor doesn't excite bees or its thicker hide protects it. Never the less, if bees were kept safe distances from farm animals and businesses, communities welcomed them for their honey, beeswax, and the pollination of fruit, nuts, berries, alfalfa and other nectar and pollen producing plants.

All bees are wild insects, but they can be modified by selective breeding. In the late 1800s Catholic Monks in Italy by selection line cross bred wild bees. Over time they produced the Italian bee. These bees were good honey producers and easy to handle. Of course, others bred bees with similar success. My bees were Italian bees and easy to manage compared with what beekeepers now must contend with due to the invasion of the Brazilian Hybrid Africanized Bee.

The Africanized bee has spread to most southern states and beyond. Fortunately many beekeepers have learned to manage this bee. And for now, requeening with gentle queens is a temporary remedy. The Africanized bees survive well, better adapted to survive parasite pressure, but they aggressively defend their nest, making them less than ideal neighbors.

I placed bees among mesquite, cat claw, and wild flowers along the Verde River. Back then my domestic bees were easy to place, as most people didn't fear them if I placed them a safe distance from livestock and homes, or behind borders of bushes or trees.

My hives in the 1970s increased over time from my first colony to 70-90 hives. And over the years these bees annually produced nearly a ton of honey, plus blocks of solar-melted beeswax for trade.

The Mysterious Queen Bee

All worker bees are female; all drones are male. Drones patrol above hives searching for a virgin queen in her maiden flight. She's a fast flyer and must be pursued for a midair mating to take place. Though dozens of drones pursue the queen, only the fastest drone can catch her to mate, losing his life in the process. It's nature's dance of life and death. It is also a dance that determines the future of the hive. In the mating, the queen receives her lifetime of sperm.

She is able to lay both fertile and unfertile eggs. Fertile eggs produce workers, unfertile eggs produce drones. Young house bees secrete flakes of beeswax with which they form hexagonal comb cells for honey, pollen storage, and brood combs.

The Bee Space

In 1852 the Reverend Lorenzo Langstroth discovered the bee space in the beehive to be 3/8 inch. In this space, bees do not glue frames to hive bodies with propolis or bridge that space with burr comb. This small space allowed beekeepers to easily remove frames from hive bodies to inspect brood and honey. Honey is removed from frames by centrifugal extraction. Empty honey frames are then returned to the hive for repair and refilling.

Consequently, the bee space gave the beekeeper the gift of inspection and honey harvesting without destroying combs and unnecessarily killing bees. It's easy to see why this Langstroth hive became popular.

Before, bees were kept in dome-shaped straw skeps or in sections of hollow logs turned up. Honey was harvested with a knife. This method was messy, often killing bees, and destroying combs. There was no way the beekeeper could inspect a hive for the queen or brood.

The Minister's Ideal Hobby

Since beekeeping is seasonal, normally from spring into fall and since beekeeping can be a hobby, like golf, fishing, or hiking, it easily fits into the church's calendar and minister's responsibilities. It's a good hobby for a minister who needs time out for rest and time to think. While tending bees, there are few interruptions.

By the way, The Reverend Lorenzo Langstroth was a beloved minister who suffered a strange melancholy. I don't know how often or for how long. When this happened his church gave him time off to rest and work with his bees.

From my perspective, it seems as if modern man is killing bees through insecticides, air pollution, and loss of environments. Will bees survive before Eco-Man arrives? I wonder.

Flowers & Bees

'The relationship between bees and flowers is a classic example of what is known as 'coevolution.' In a coevolutionary bargain like the one struck by bees and the apple tree, the two parties act on each other to advance their individual interests, but wind up trading favors: food for the bee, transportation for the apple genes. Consciousness needn't enter into it on either side, or the traditional distinction between the subject and object is meaningless."

The Botany of Desire by Michael Pollan

Coevolution is complicated. Simplicity—an innocent child looks at a bee and a flower and knows only a bee and flower.

Written in 2017. A version of "Musings of a Beekeeping Minister" was published in the May 2018 issue of *The American Bee Journal.*

My Money Tree

I once had a money tree, a birthday gift from my first born daughter, Dianna. This money tree, growing from a beautiful pot, had a four-stem braided trunk. It once lived in my living room before a window with Venetian blinds half closed. It liked half light, I'm told, mostly shade, and water now and then. It also liked me to mist its leaves each day which leads me to believe its ancestors lived in a warm, humid climate. When I do, it feels at home, a contented living thing. How do I know how this plant felt? I studied and imagined it.

It was the only green growing life in my home. No other house plant distracted me. I studied its dollar shaped leaves and thought: If I had hoped of financial return, it was a bad investment; however, if I measured its worth in another coin, I was rich.

Beginning in 1968 with an acre of irrigated land through five decades to 2015, Doris and I enjoyed at least 70 trees: Arizona Cypress, Mondale Pine, locust, and mulberry to name a few. Also we lived with apple, peach, apricot, plum, and a male cherry tree. The cherry was male, just a pet.

We included grapevines, a vegetable garden, flowers and roses that bloomed here and there. We kept six beehives at home surrounded by trees, which protected neighbors. Some got in our house. You could say we lived with bees.

Also I kept 70-90 hives up and down the Verde River. Looking back I'm amazed we managed all this, while leading a church congregation and active in community service. We had the amazing gifts of health and youth.

During the honey season, usually on a Saturday, we scheduled visits for Head Start and grade school children with their teachers and aides to our apiary and honey extracting room.

Safe behind trellised grapevines and trees, with openings they could peek through, they watched me open a hive and show them a frame of honey.

Then we visited our honey extracting room. As planned, Doris had baked biscuits for the visit. For each student we dipped honey from a saucer on each biscuit. A pail of water stood close for washing hands afterwards.

On one visit, all the children but one moved out of the honey room. I looked back and saw a small boy with his hands cupped under the wide open valve of our full thirty-gallon honey tank. His hands were full and honey was flowing to the floor. I rushed back and turned off the valve, then plunged his hands in the bucket of water (and cleaned the floor later). When small children visited, it was always good to laugh a lot and always look back.

My money tree not only reminded me of our flora and fauna sanctuary, it also reminded me of the many visitors who came and enjoyed our acre and had a bee experience.

This single money tree that once lived in my living room, silently reminded me of my Doris who passed on five years ago. I remember our wealth of a different kind, a green, animal, insect acre of life that money can't buy.

Unlike paper and digital money lost in spending and theft, I can replace my money tree with its memories. Now is the time to buy another one and set it before a shaded window in my living room.

I no longer live in that acre; I'm too far along in years. I moved and live in town.

Written in 2015.

Born Wild

She was a puppy wandering the dangerous blacktop of a fast traffic road; just a frightened little animal zigzagging a nowhere path down the middle of danger.

How she got there I will never know, but it was certain she would soon lose her life if she remained there long. I stopped, scooped her into my car, and from that moment she was my dog.

We named her Christmas after the season I found her. And in the seasons and years that followed she grew from a puppy in a box in the barn to our yard, and then to the big outdoors.

Christmas was always our friend, never our pet. She belonged to the wild. We tried to tame her, but she always found a way to be free. She feared the chain that caught her spirit and sapped her strength link by link. She hated the limits of our acre, and like a prisoner, she fought the fence, dug tunnels, and won.

One day I found her lying near death in a roadside ditch. She had been scavenging road-kill rabbits when a car hit her. Our vet sewed her face together and I nursed her back to health.

One night, after missing her for several days, I heard her whining in the barn. I searched and found her in the shadows. Drawing close I saw that her front paw was caught in a coyote trap. The trap's chain was still wired to a stake. Apparently she had lunged against the stake until it had pulled loose and set her free. Only God knows how long it took to do that but I guessed at least a couple of days and nights. I carefully removed the trap, dressed her paw, carried food and water to her until she healed. For a long time after she was a perfect yard dog.

Seasons passed into dog-years. Though old, Christmas was still young in heart and continued to hate the chain and fight the fence. Once she heard the call of the wild and escaped into the night. I heard her barking and howling with the coyotes in the hills, and I wondered how long before they turned on her and brought her down. More importantly, I worried that she would join a pack of feral dogs and do dark mischief, or suffer a slow death in another trap.

One summer morning, after a new day broke open and released its yellow sun, and after warm light had streamed through my bedroom window, I rose from a sleepless night. All through the night I had argued my case in my court of conscience. When morning broke I had my verdict. I had reached a conclusion through compelling evidence, compassion, and reason. A countdown began.

When my time comes to go, I want to leave this world quick and merciful, like a dove by hawk, or a deer by fang and claw. I want to go with innocent trust in my Master's quick touch—a sudden gift of God. But seldom is this granted humans by humans. Our departure is usually a slow sedated passage by medicine's soft-cross. This we know, it may be years of pharmaceutical intervention, by Hospice care, then finally by life ticking into hours with monitors digitizing medicine into days. This can't be otherwise for religion, conscience, and compassionate laws join science to lift us above the wild kingdom. So precious is human life we dare not destroy it, not without compelling reason.

In her innocent trust, Christmas had no way of knowing what the morning meant for her. She yawned and slowly rose on arthritic legs. I leashed her collar and together we went to the wilderness where important matters are decided and make sense. Here is a wild wholeness that escapes our civil ideals. Here, her wolf ancestors lived, thrived, and died. Here is where predator and prey live side by side in birth and death without guilt and regret. It cannot be otherwise.

When evening fell, we both returned home.

A version of "Born Wild" was published *as* "The Gift"
in the *Verde View,* August 10, 1979

The Rattle Snake

A Rattlesnake crawled,
From under the night,
Plugged in its coil,
To the heat of a rock,
Charged up its venom,
For sudden strike.

A dinner bell moon,
Called a kangaroo rat,
The snake unplugged
With a sparkly flash,
Traded its breakfast,
For a midnight snack.

Being a snake, it was cold-blooded. Cold nights drained its warmth and a mid-day sun scorched the sand to near death. Fortunately, this snake found relief under the shadow of a sage bush, then squirmed into sand; its diamond back made it invisible to most.

As the day heated, it squirmed deeper into cooling sand and debris, all the while moving the rat along its digestive track.

Now and then the snake's darting tongue searched, and sifted the air and tasted whiffs of greasewood and rodent hair.

The snake knew its predator-place in nature and adapted to it. Though most animals feared it and fled its terrible poison, it too was prey. This snake must watch for hawks, eagles, and javelina; consequently, forced to live by stealth and terror, which made its desert life a lonely one. Fortunately, though, in its lonely isolation, this serpent enjoyed its outcast's solitary peace — a hermit's peace.

Suddenly, it sensed a slight disturbance in the desert's wholeness. First, there was only a slight tugging of the desert's fabric. The snake squirmed deeper into its hiding place. Something was coming through the desert toward him and the snake sensed an ancient foe and prepared for battle. It armed its fangs and cocked its head, while terrible poison swelled, ready to deal the intruder cell-destroying pain and nerve-toxin death. The battleground had been well chosen; the advantage was the snake's.

A first strike lay in secrecy and surprise. The battle was about to begin. The intruder was now within striking distance when something in the serpent's heart spoke mercy. In that moment the snake threw away its advantage with a warning buzz. That warning triggers fear in all creatures, but often means the snake's doom. Easily the snake could have sunk its twin fangs deep in human flesh. He could have won the first round of the battle.

Instantly, the snake's warning pumped adrenalin's fear and triggered my reflex jump and I cleared that cocked head. Fear cascaded over reason and every cell screamed attack. Quickly I raised my walking stick to beat this dreaded thing back to earth. But then, almost too late, a small voice spoke, "Should this snake be more merciful than you? What harm would come in this wild place far from beaten path if you let this snake live? Is there not a place where ancient enemies can meet in peace?" The answer came in the snake's return to its hermit peace and my fading footfalls. The desert was whole again.

A version was published in the *Verde View,* August 15, 1978

Scott and Linda Dieringer

The scent of fresh leather, the spicy smell preservatives, and the friendly busyness of the family gave the building an Old West welcome.

Scott Dieringer became interested in leather while still a boy of twelve living in his home state of Washington. Beginning as a hobby craft, he made the usual belts and wallets, learned basic skills on fresh leather and discovered the satisfaction of turning good leather into useful items.

Later, he hired out as a cowboy on a working ranch, taking off a month or so each year during the slow season to work for Saddles of Pendleton. He cleaned up, swept out, and did odd jobs just for the privilege of learning the trade— no pay. He also studied under the respected saddlemaker, Claude Mills of High River, Alberta, Canada.

Scott and Linda married in 1966 and moved to Camp Verde 14 years ago. Their saddlery business provides ranch hands and horse fanciers with quality leather goods, old fashioned craftsmanship and an inventory of tack. The family worked in a rented building on Main Street until they built their own saddle shop on the access road just south of the town. It is said by those who helped build the family's new home and saddlery that Linda could handle woodworking tools and cut a straight line through plywood as well as anyone—figures.

Scott and Linda brought three children into the world: Chamita, Sam and Chet. This business is a family business, which means there's something for everyone to do. Scott does the heavy work and stitching, Linda does the full flower carving on most of the saddles. A wood burning stove in the center of the room not only warms, it also gives the building its special cedar and oak wood smells.

Any cowhand coming in from a cow outfit will find Scott's Saddlery welcoming. It's a place where the Scott Dieringer family works together as people worked a century ago.

Last Saturday, I visited Scott's and Linda's saddlery and found the family busy at work. Chet, the youngest son, was busy tearing down an old saddle and was carefully cutting each stitch from the old leather, getting it ready for repair. The other members worked at more complicated jobs.

I had to ask, "Who's in charge?" Scott gave me his big outdoor smile and tossed this answer in my direction: "It depends on what day it is." Linda chuckled and looked up from behind her work bench. Chet grinned like his father.

I know why this family business works for them. The family supplies customers with tack, tarps, and custom-made belts and holsters. Lariats hang coiled from ceiling hooks, while two Idaho willow chairs recently laced with rawhide and leather wait their owners.

A St. Louis tannery supplies Scott and Linda with saddle leather. This particular tannery still uses the old fashioned oak and barks methods of tanning, a method that has earned the respect and confidence of active outdoor people. Scott gets his saddletrees from five different places, mostly from Kenny Hawes of Moab, Utah. Scott's saddles go to Germany, Australia, Texas, Nevada, Montana, California, and New Mexico; although much of this family's handiwork stays in Arizona furnishing local working ranches and horse breeders with reliable leather goods.

Obviously, the family is well endowed with faith, a healthy work ethic, and self-reliance. Scott told me that when they moved into their new home, they left their TV disconnected, and now the family has become accustomed to not having one. The children read more books, and their recreation time is spent moving about in the forest, camping under ponderosa pines.

Scott hunts mountain lions with dogs when his rancher friends need help hunting a lion whose preference turns from deer to beef. When this call of the wild becomes more urgent than his need to make saddles, he will disappear into the outback.

The family is also involved in their community. The Chemical People (illegal drugs) program has their support, and when school or summer activities make their rounds, you'll see them supporting youth programs and cheering for their home teams.

Wonderfully, the Scott and Linda family does not suffer the attention of police, is drug free, out of debt, and very good citizens. The Dieringer family is a respected addition to the Camp Verde community.

A version of "Scott and Linda Dieringer" was published in *The Journal*, December 14, 1983.

Cowboys, Horses, Cattle, and Lions

The big tom mountain lion knew not the logic of cattle ranch business, only his need to eat. He was hungry. Beef was good and easy to catch.

Scott Dieringer and Bobby Reeves hunt mountain lions that turn from deer to cattle killing. If a rancher finds fresh lion-kill, Scott and Bobby hunt that lion by horseback with Scott's dogs working the lion scent. They'd follow their lion through rugged canyons and along mountain ridges of Arizona, then tree it or run it out of the country. They prefer the tree.

The moon cast its night glow over the meadow and long shadows spread from mountain ridges and clumps of cottonwood trees. The big tom lion slipped down from a ridge of rocks and followed a shadow finger to where the cattle waited.

Nervous mother cows called their calves close; an old bull snorted and pawed the ground in fear and anger. The restless herd waited for what was coming as their ancestors had waited for the coming of wolves and lions in their nights. This had always been the way of bison, wolves and lions.

These cattle knew the way of mountain lions that came for their sick, old, and calves, and they knew how to protect themselves. If they stayed together, the lion would move on to easier prey; however, if a cow in labor had wandered too far from the herd, a lion may try to kill her.

The lion would not attack the old bull—too risky. He had to be careful to not let the old bull cripple him. A horn or hoof might break his jaw or leg, or blind him. These wounds would tip the scales against his survival. He preferred a calf, heifer or steer.

The lion found a young steer bathed in moonlight at the edge of the herd. Squalling and snarling he launched a running attack, leaped on the steer, and bit into its neck, then finished his kill with a strangle hold on its throat. The herd scattered into the night. The lion dragged the steer into a grove of trees, ate the liver, lungs and heart and left the rest for another day. After a week, he would be back for another beef dinner.

Domesticated cattle have had their survival tools compromised by centuries of selective breeding to satisfy easier handling, faster weight gain, and tender table meat.

Nature, however, for millennia favored dangerous mothers and brave bulls, both with long, sharp horns, nimble legs, and sharp hooves. Now, too much taming old cowboys say. Of course, few want to turn back the clock.

Easy to see, there is a necessary predator side of wild life. Although the table manners of wolves are disgusting and cruel by our standards—eating prey while still alive, they do play an important role in the Wild Kingdom.

Aside from vegans and vegetarians, we are also predators and carnivores. Though not eating from Nature's raw table, our cattle killing is out of sight in slaughter houses and meat is eaten with polite table manners in restaurants or burger businesses.

Last week Scott Dieringer and Bobby Reeves legally hunted a beef-killing lion over by Cordes Junction.

A version of "Cowboys, Horses, Cattle and Lions" was published in
The Journal in 1984.

Dave Murdoch

Longtime friends and family gathered at the Clear Creek Cemetery to say farewell to Dave Murdock, a gentleman father, a citizen, a pioneer, an old time cowboy of Camp Verde. July, 1886—1983.

We all said good-bye to a legend. We don't have many of them anymore.

Dave lived 96 years before his Creator called him home last week. He lived most of his 96 years close to nature and the land that he loved.

Dave was born in Medicine Lodge, Kansas, July 22, 1886. His family decided to travel by horse and wagon to the Verde Valley, Arizona. At the age of four Dave rode his horse behind his family wagon. Can you imagine a four-year-old riding a horse from Kansas to Arizona?

Dave married Kathleen McDonald, affectingly known as Lena in 1915, and their first home was what is now the Fort Verde Museum. They brought into the world 12 children, 10 now living. They are survived by 41 grandchildren and 42 great-grandchildren.

Dave was a cowboy of that proud tradition unknown by the present standards so popularized in the entrainment media. He didn't hang around saloons picking fights. He didn't gun down people in the middle of streets, nor did he throw people through barroom windows.

He was something of a loner at times. He enjoyed the company of a few good friends, cared for his family and spent a lot of time working his cattle. The old days were his days, and when the times began to change, he stayed the same.

It can be said of Dave, even in his last days, he was tough as rawhide but remained to the end a Victorian gentleman, as gentle and kind as he was strong.

I can see him now. I see his big smile and the firm strength in his handshake. It became increasingly difficult for him to sit a horse, for much of his strength had turned inward for that last ditch battle in the winter of his life. Like a great oak tree shelters its life-strength down deep in its roots, he remained active, even though his bones had become dry and brittle and his joints stiff and sore. He still moved like a man half his age.

Dave's eyes became dim, so dim he gave up driving his car and found other ways to get to town. He drove his tractor and was often seen leading a parade of cars across the White Bridge and up into town. Those who knew him were patient, but newcomers who brought so much hurry from the fast pace they left behind angrily honked their horns. However, this man who as a boy of four rode a horse from Kansas to Arizona wasn't going to be hurried by honking horns.

Soon, however, even the tractor was too much for his failing sight, and Dave was left with his horse. The horse could see well enough for both of them. Dave hung in there even when his options diminished one by one. In my travels around town I would see him helping someone who needed a helping hand.

Dave Murdock's ranch extended from meander land along the Verde River to the hills above Camp Verde. He ran cattle under the Dart Bar brand. In those days Dave's cattle moved at will in this open range and that included the village of Camp Verde. Cattlemen and pioneers understood the need for open range laws, but newcomers did not know the need or chose to ignore it.

It was common to wake in the middle of the night to sounds of Dart-Bar cattle grazing on your front lawn. If you wanted to keep out Dave's cows, you had to fence them out. That was the law. Cattle guards were installed, but Dave's cows learned to jump them. Fences were built and strengthened, but Dave's bulls knew how to walk through barbed wire as they walked through cat's claw and mesquite thickets. Dave's cows hung in there, but the town grew and changed and people with different concerns came to stay. And these people from cities and farmlands knew only Western movie and paperback cowboys.

For these people unbridled, semi-wild cattle freely roaming proved too much. Many were afraid. Phone calls in the middle of the night told him, "Your cows are eating my garden." Dave replied, "That's OK, your corn shouldn't hurt them much." This range war of words continued between the town and Dave until Dave no longer ran cows. What the sparse land, summer drought, and screw worm failed to do, modern progress did. Dave and his cows parted. An era ended.

Dave was one with the land he loved. He knew the cry of the coyote, a mother cow calling her calf. He knew the challenging bellows of bulls and the dust, dirt, and sweat of roundup and branding time. He left the job of cutting out young stock and gave others the fire and Dart-Bar branding iron.

Dave was the best part of the Old West that is fast disappearing. There will always be cattle, for people like beef, but the ways of managing cattle today has become computerized and mechanized. Cowboys like Dave are no longer needed—so they say. The newcomer invasion of the West changed everything, everything but Dave Murdock.

This is the day we remember and honor Dave Murdoch. He knew the call of the owl when they called his name. Last week they called his name for the last time.

Written in 1983.

Mr. Gardner's Kellogg Job

"The more one forgets himself—by giving himself to a cause to serve or another person to love—the more human he is and the more he actualizes himself." Victor Frankl, *Man's Search for Meaning.*

It was the Great Depression and hard times for many fathers who scratched a bare-bones living, often supplemented by government commodities, mostly prunes and corn meal, sometimes grapefruit. To this day, I clean my plate and wince when I see good food become instant garbage.

Children remember families. One stands out for me. It was the Gardner family. At least half a dozen claimed family resemblance and a dozen or so neighborhood strays claimed the Gardner hospitality. I was one of them. Their screen door constantly batted to the tempo of kid-life.

Furthermore, Mr. Gardner rested securely in his Kellogg's of Battle Creek job. This good man smelled of cereal and to this day, when I sniff an open box of Corn Flakes, I remember him. Mr. Gardner also smoked—he smoked hard! At the time it was OK. When I smell tobacco, I think of him.

The Gardner family was a good neighbor and for us kids the family was a friendly gathering place for fun and food. Good times had come for us kids and would come again for our country. We never gave up hope.

Mr. Gardner could afford the fruitful love of Mrs. Gardner, a pleasingly plump woman with a smile as open and warm as baked bread just broken; in contrast, Mr.

Gardner's smile was a cadaverous crack in his parchment face. To this day, I'm amazed at how much life sprang from this graveyard of a man.

Evenings, we sat around the Gardner's radio and listened to *The Lone Ranger*, while spreading peanut butter on thick slices of homemade bread. Then Mr. Gardner separated us out, sent neighborhood strays home and kept those that resembled him.

Written in 2000.

Rena Frew

"If you have anything to contribute to the world it still comes through the expression of your own personality."
Bruce Barton

Like a pioneer woman traveling West in a covered wagon, Rena Frew travels long distances in her self-contained van.

It's OK to be different. We don't need to be the same size, look alike, think alike, and do the same things in order to be alright. In fact, reasonable, appropriate, and harmonizing is built into life's differences. Obviously, there are two major divisions among us: male and female, which gives us unique differences and fascinating relationships.

Rena Frew of Camp Verde, Arizona is amazingly different. This woman is four-foot, eight inches tall; although it is insensitive to estimate a woman's weight, I invite censor by judging her to be between eighty and one hundred pounds. But let not anyone underestimate the strength, intellect and spirituality of this woman. She's a half-pint, full-gallon woman.

Rena earned her B.A. degree at Geneva College, and won her Master's at Michigan State. She spent sixteen years of her professional life teaching junior high physical education. She speaks of spending every school day in the gym directing the exercises and games of ninety boys and girls. She was also a special education teacher for eighteen years and a professional Girl Scout leader for ten.

She was given a scholarship by The Ninety-Nines, a woman's flying society, for a course in Airspace Education at the Miami University of Ohio. She was also involved in training a squadron of cadets and was a member of the Civil Air Patrol, flying as an observer over wilderness areas in California looking for downed planes and lost people. Rena's scholarship and volunteer accomplishments if listed vertically would reach higher then most of us stand tall.

After her retirement in 1971, she helped the Arizona Game and Fish department keep track of Big Horn Sheep; wild life biologists were interested in the count of ewes, lambs, quarter curl, half curl, and full curl rams. She hiked into their mountain habitats to count the Big Horn sheep.

Rena continues to be different and very busy. In church, she cares for children while their parents attend choir practice, serves as Sunday School Superintendent for the church, and is an active member of the Senior Center in Camp Verde. There she keeps a careful watch over seniors who are often ten years her junior. She also cares for the small pioneer cemetery next to the Center. This little cemetery is the burial grounds for four people who died during the Camp Verde flood in 1905, which prevented their burial at the Clear Creek Cemetery.

By the way, she will be seventy-nine this year and shows no sign of running out of things to do. I asked her what's the worst thing about growing old. She said, "The only thing wrong about being old is that people don't need you anymore." She must have picked it up while listening to her peers.

I can't imagine the time when she won't be needed.

A version of "Rena Frew" was published in *The Journal* in 1984.

Carl Goswick

Carl Goswick was a mentally-challenged adult living in Camp Verde, Arizona. You would see him moving shopping carts around and helping people with their groceries at Camp Verde's Fairway General Store, or perhaps he would be a doorman greeting customers at the town's only drugstore. Carl volunteered his service and would not accept tips. Sometimes Fairway gave him a birthday or Christmas present, perhaps a Western shirt and pair of pants, but that's all, unless you count job satisfaction.

He helped customers park their cars, although this service was discouraged by the Fairway manger after a lady whom Carl thought was illegally parking, took exception to his helpful criticism and hit him with her purse.

Carl was born in Camp Verde, Arizona on June 26, 1922, to Louise and Bill Goswick. Louise was unable to nurse Carl and the milk substitute of that day was rejected by baby Carl. Malnourished, he weakened and began to die. Toward the end, he was but a tiny skeleton resting in the middle of a soft pillow. In desperate hope, he was wet-nursed by his aunt. Mother's milk was what his little body needed. Carl began to recover, gained weight, and grew into a strong, healthy boy; however, as family members suspect, during his near-death experience, something important to him was missing. During those early critical weeks, what he needed for coping in this complex world had died.

Finally, when Carl grew several heads taller than his classmates and still couldn't keep up with them, Carl's mother took him out of the Camp Verde Grade School. There were no Special Ed Programs and no sheltered workshops then; therefore, Carl stayed home and worked with his father on the ranch.

How could he understand his loss of what he never had? He could only know by comparing himself with those who were better endowed. Such a life was given. Frustrated and with soft anger, Carl lived a good life in spite of his lot in life. Carl coped extremely well.

Carl was an only child and when his father died, he faithfully cared for his mother until she passed away a number of years ago. On a wood stove he cooked five meals a day, helped his mother move about during her invalid days, and ran his mother's errands. She would give him a grocery list and enough money. He trustingly gave the list and money to the clerk at Wingfield's General Store. The list would then be serviced and the right change given back. It takes a lot of faith to live in Carl's world, and it takes a lot of trustworthy people to make it happen.

Carl's father once was a deputy sheriff and Carl thought the job was hereditary. To add authority to this misunderstanding, he carried the County Sheriff's business card in his wallet. He thought this card gave him the right to enforce the law, especially intervene in fights. Consequently, Carl was involved in dangerous incidents before he was transferred from law enforcement to crime reporting. Carl was promoted to calling the Sheriff if he saw trouble. Not a bad job for the rest of us.

Those who don't know Carl, newcomers in particular, don't understand why he volunteers his services free of charge—no tips. Why not? Simply put, Carl was caught in a Catch-22. If he received money for his work, he would have lost his State of Arizona financial support. If Carl lost his state support, which he needed for his survival, he would be lost in a world suddenly too complex and too bewildering for words. Carl's mother knew this and warned him to never to take money for his work and being a good son he obeyed his mother.

Carl's distant relatives help him. Janie Kilby does his correspondence and Evelyn and Clint Wager supervises his diet and personal hygiene. Pastor Dwight Bowser was his spiritual mentor and I managed his single hive of bees in his back yard.

Time, schedules, social interaction, and math are beyond him. But he does excel in simple things, the value of which often escapes the more gifted. He knows the pleasure of helping others, even if no paycheck is in the picture. He knows his place in the big picture and works at it. Although he won't ever own a business, discover a cure for cancer, or have wife and family, he won't invent new ways to deliver hydrogen bombs, threaten the environment with toxic chemical, or bring children into the world only to abandon them when he tires of their mother. Once more, it's not people like Carl who manage to mess up life on a grand scale—it's usually gifted people with degrees.

Postscript: While I served a church in Patagonia, Arizona, this tragic story unfolded: one night two men broke into Carl Goswick's home to rob him of his money and collection of Kachina dolls. He had none, but these men didn't know that. Finding no money or Kachina dolls, they beat Carl to death. The police said it was a robbery gone wrong. The good people of Camp Verde suspected local men; however, the police were unable to tie them to the murder. There were neither suspects nor leads. The Carl Goswick murder case grew cold and now is buried in an unsolved crime file.

But you can't kill a man like Carl by beating the life out of him. That life merely escapes a mortal body. Carl now lives in the collective memory of the good folks of Camp Verde, in the consciences of his killers, and in the loving care of The Almighty.

I believe his new body will be wondrously whole and perfectly blessed with a gift of intelligence that will be out of this world.

A version of "Carl Goswick" was published in
The Journal, October 12, 1983.

Hospital Housekeeping

Seldom do we think of that small band of housekeepers who make healing places possible.

I watched a Verde Valley Medical Center housekeeper, supplied from her scrub-down cart, clean a hospital room. She moved quickly and methodically to get her work done on a tight time schedule. She had other rooms to clean before this day's end.

It takes focused time and hard work to do it right. She had to scrub and wipe all surfaces with strong germ and virus killing disinfectants. Nothing must remain that will make the next patient sick. Although she easily disinfected hard surfaces, resistant germs and viruses hide deep in seams and creases and only die by hard scrubbing. Deep scrubbing she did.

When we think of hospitals, we usually think a long list of office staff, doctors, nurses, technology, technicians, labs, patients, and volunteers. Flashing lights and sirens of ambulances demand our attention, too. Seldom do we think of that small band of housekeepers who make healing places possible. They are low-profile persons. Few of us know their names; some know what they do. They drift barely visible through hospital halls and in and out of rooms. People look but don't see.

They seldom if ever receive awards or newspaper coverage, unless they've served the best of their years and retire. Nevertheless, without them the modern hospital could not do its healing work. Diseases more deadly than those in streets and homes would stalk hospital rooms, equipment, beds, and surgical bays, thus undoing the healing arts and successes of professional healers.

There was a time in the not distant past when germs and viruses were unknown. The French microbiologist Louis Pasteur (1822-1895) unmasked the hospital's infectious enemy. Joseph Lister (1827-1912), applied the discoveries of Pasteur. He used a disinfectant tincture of carbolic acid in his practice. The story is told: Doctor Lister placed a pail of his carbolic mixture at the door of the autopsy room and instructed his doctors to use it. But some doctors ignored the pail and walked straight from autopsy to surgery and maternity without washing their hands. It was no wonder that people knew hospital surgery was a death sentence and women chose home births and midwives instead of hospitals. But soon, irrefutable evidence persuaded even the most reluctant to use Lister's pail of carbolic mixture.

A lesson from a page in Nature: nature's basic food source, flora, through millenniums developed toxins, poisons, and behaviors as defenses against hungry animals, infections, and insects, all which could decrease their survival.

Human and other animal-based bodies have their gifts of housekeeping immune systems that have kept them ahead of mutating germs and viruses.

For humans, moving from farms to small towns to cities made contagion easier. Fortunately, after each endemic, epidemic and pandemic enough of us survived to repopulate.

Nature's housekeeping examples are easily known. Definitely, the most efficient disease control known is forest and habitat fire. It kills insects, disease carrying dead trees, brush and human habitation. Cities burned down. If left unburned, forests and habitats would provide permanent sanctuary to diseases.

Vulture and buzzard's gastric juices disarm even the dreaded anthrax disease, rendering it non-contagious. There is a long list of Nature's housekeeping scavengers, unknown to most. Not only do these housekeepers recycle the dead, they make life possible on planet earth.

Domestic and wild honey bee colonies are immaculate housekeepers. They clean each nursery cell before and after use. House bees clean internal surfaces and carry dead bees safe distances from their hives. They won't allow the accumulation of waste in their hives. Furthermore, they paint the walls of their hives-with mildly antiseptic propolis. These housekeepers are as important to the hive as guards, scouts, nectar and pollen foragers. Over millions of years, honey bees have mutated and kept ahead of their diseases.

I could go on and on with examples of human and natural housekeeping and every example proves that life as we know it depends on good housekeeping.

Hats off to that small band of House Keepers now serving the Verde Valley Medical Center.

Chaplain John W. Jenkins

A version of "Hospital Housekeeping" was published as "Housekeeping Far From Routine at Laurence Memorial Hospital" in *The Journal*, January 10, 1984. Revised 2017.

Naturally

This is fun-time for poking fun at normal people who eat normal food without guilt and for food purists, and the rest of us, who have neurotic food scruples. That said, let's begin.

The definition of junk food will vary with the person and locality. What is "junk" and "fast" food for one person is a fast-served gastronomical treasure to another.

Food purists insist that our food must always be healthy and nutritious. I almost agree with that. To meet these requirements, they insist our food must come straight from field, garden, tree and vine, and be free of insecticides, pesticides, herbicides, and industrial wastes. Also it must be free of excessive fat, salt, and empty calories. Who can argue with that? Lots of people do.

Food purists also insist our food is better jerked, dried, caked, compressed, and reduced to its basic components. It's even better if our meals are garnished with herbal supplements.

If food tastes strangely foreign, sour, nutty, dry, and vinegary, it must be good. Yogurt leads the list because it resembles anemic pudding and tastes like sour milk. This isn't something the normal person craves when hankering for a tallow-flavored burger and salty French fries.

I confess sometimes I'm tempted to go over to the dark side. It must be my grandfather's genes acting up. I'm in good company. The ultramarathon cyclist Lon Haldeman was seen by millions eating pizza and confessed to having a taste for fast food burgers. What's worse, many saw him eating fast food while leading the bike pack. Health food purists cringe when they see outstanding athletes eat like everyone else. Not eating at a health food bar for the purist is like missing Mass for a good Catholic.

Our iconic naturalist, John Muir broke our modern health food rules with a passion. He can't be blamed, for he lived before health food laws and politically correct food police. Not to worry, he's grandfathered in. This founder and president of the Sierra Club was so free of food anxiety all he needed for a trip into the mountains was a sack of stale bread and tea along with what he could find. (He did not carry a sleeping bag nor a gun.) He stayed in the mountains until his simple diet was gone. Not many like him around anymore. Super food people can't allow this obvious exception to deter them from their diets and meddling with ours.

Defecting to the other side, it's not fast food, its fast service that's provided. It's convenient food for those who wait in the hurry lines at take-out windows.

Fast food is usually nutritious and reasonable healthy, though too greasy and salty for me. People become overweight not by eating fast food; they just eat too much of it. There, now, I am redeemed.

I confess I'm a vegetarian most of the time—not vegan, although I respect those who are. I'm silent about my diet and grateful for what is set before me while eating at other tables. I read somewhere that the vegan Dalai Lama was seen eating meat at a dinner gathering and was criticized by a disciple. His gentle rebuke: "This meat is dead, my host is alive." I like that answer. Also I read somewhere that the Dalai Lama's doctor recommended some meat. He now eats some chicken. That's almost meat.

Now and then I have a green chili burro with jalapeno peppers, a hotdog, or a hamburger with fries, all without guilt. This redeems me from self-righteousness and food fascism. Remember Seinfeld's Soup Nazi?

My usual breakfast is a cup of coffee, a half-cup of cooked quinoa with raisins, dried cranberries, a handful of almonds, sunflower seeds, pumpkin seeds, a pinch of salt and, if facing a busy day, two spoons of flaxseed meal in a glass of orange juice. Other times just nuts, an apple and banana. Wow. I just surprised myself with how good I am.

I know that our recent and distant ancestors, rich and poor alike, ate what was available and affordable, most often unhealthy choices. Think road kill and items on the forbidden Hebrew menu. Think eating each other. Think moldy insect-infested flour, plus time-challenged sea food. They didn't have good nutrition science, nor the benefits of a sanitary food chain. Think Upton Sinclair's 1906 novel, *The Jungle*.

However they did have salt for preserving cod fish at sea. They had ice for trains, cellars for milk and cheese. Plus frozen meat in northern winters, smoke houses for farm and game animals, plus canned food put up from their own harvest.

Now, we have global food flown to market the same day of harvest and food inspectors watching out for us. In case you wonder, facilities are provided for field workers. Unfortunately hepatitis and gastrointestinal diseases will sneak through; therefore wash veggies and cook meat past pink. Predators like the sight and taste of blood.

Now, we have computerized surgery, multi-million-dollar diagnostic machines, chemo and radiation, along with smart doctors, vaccines, and better sanitation. We now have Big Pharma's antibiotics and hormonal pantry. And we now have prescription drugs that wake up sleepy hearts and jump-start libido's sex drive.

More of us will live into our nineties and beyond; I'm concerned about that benefit. My ancestors ate, smoked, chewed, and intoxicated themselves to heart's content; not without the body's revenge. Though they left the good earth in their twenties, thirties, and forties, too young to suffer many diseases and disabilities we now suffer.

All our lifesaving goodies come with escalating health costs. Some worry that our health maintenance and insurance may bankrupt the country. That's a political and financial can we kick down the road.

Now, we no longer need to worry about leaving inheritances to wayward offspring, for we now have time to spend it all. However, those of us who grew up during The Great Depression tend to be neurotic plate cleaners and habitual savers. Consequently, spending it all may not be an option.

Written in 2010.

Send in the Clowns

The circus comes to town and people respond according to their conditioning and interest. Some are disinterested, while others are enthusiastic, especially children and childlike adults.

Clowns and apes, elephants and lions, tigers and leopards, bears and horses perform in the ring. A performer walks a thin wire stretched too far, too high.

Clowns come laughing and skipping, falling and dancing. They are playful children, foolish in their wisdom, simple in their complexity, clumsy in their grace, and prankish in their play.

Clowns bring laughter. It's hard to take the circus too seriously when the clowns come in. Clowns soften risk and danger. Clowns rush in where we fear to go. Clowns—no harm in them—exaggerate our humanity. They paint their faces white, black, and color. They grin, laugh, frown, and cry too much. Their baggy pants, floppy shoes, funny hats, stumbling gaits poke fun at fashion and invite us to laugh at ourselves.

May I suggest some relationships between playful clowns and the clergy. The clergy, like clowns, take upon themselves our humanity and show us how to cry and laugh, sing and dance, stumble, flop, fall, then get up and continue on.

Stevens Gimble: "Once Einstein was at a film premier with Charlie Chaplain and the crowd went wild. Charlie explained to Einstein what was going on. They cheer me because they understand me, and they cheer you because no one understands you."

Written in 1994.

Itch and Scratch

My thoughts turn to a friend's small dog named Patches. When she sees me coming, she wiggles and dances for she knows I'll give her a good scratch at the base of her tail. She's in dog heaven with her head turned up, her lips in open smile. If I were itchy Patches being scratched at the base of my tail, that would be my big scratch. I wouldn't trade it for a gold mine nor a million dollar lottery win.

A longing for adventure is an itch, curiosity is another. The hunger and thirst for knowledge is an itch and the scratch is learning beyond what's known.

Also, experience is an itch and wisdom is its scratch. Unrequited love is an itch and finding true love is the big scratch—big time. And to believe that the earth holds treasure just waiting to be found is a deep itch; how wonderful is the scratch when found.

Nevada has ghost towns with abandoned gold and silver mines. Long ago, men and women, and families with children bet their lives, time, labor, and savings on mining claims hoping to find their fortune. But few found enough gold and silver to make them neither content nor rich. Most miners dug and found only broken dreams and poverty, lots of itch, little scratch. Though they had big itches and few scratches, not all was lost. Though they had screwed up their lives, they had fun doing it. Not a bad trade.

I believe high adventure and impossible dreams against great odds is an itch and scratch combined. It gives our lives meaning. Our Father in heaven knows what's best.

Let's consider Lady Luck. Now, there's an itchy lady and if she scratches with a big win, you gotta keep that lady around, even though we know she's married to the casino manager.

True believers in Lady Luck believe that a million dollar scratch will come someday. That's their itch that keeps on itching. But then, wonder of wonders, the gamer hits the jackpot and wins big. The winner of a million dollar lottery ticket has a big scratch. That's one big scratch for humans, but not for Patches-dog.

Instead of Lady Luck, some folks believe God gives special scratches to favorite people. I wonder and suggest God is more like an umpire than Lady Luck. For those who believe God favors them with big scratches, it is like asking God to give their favorite baseball team a win at the expense of a loser. I suggest a team's big scratch depends on team training, practice, will to win, team cohesion, and individual skills, plus that bouncing ball joker card of random chance. These wins and loses are embedded in life. I suggest God throws these in just to keep the game of life interesting.

In baseball, how the ball comes off the bat, where it bounces, and when the sun blinds an outfielder can determine a winner or loser.

Our itchy desire for perfection and our itchy imperfection welcomes a good winning scratch now and then; it's embedded in the game of life, too. Those who bat 300 out of a 1,000 are winners and heroes. That's the most we can hope for in baseball.

I'm convinced God is more interested in our itchy faith, hope, and love—wisdom too, and gives special scratches when practiced.

In conclusion, I now remember Doris; sweet and sad memories float to the surface of memories. For instance, memories of our bicycle and camper tour across America shore to shore. I rode my bicycle; she was my backup. It was not a race. Wonderfully, each day along the way we had time to visit interesting places and people. We then had a month to visit our daughter and her family in Virginia Beach and explore Washington, D.C.

The trip across America by bicycle and camper, following the Bikecentennial Route on the TransAmerica Bicycle Trail was our big scratch. It was our second honeymoon.

Written in 2017.

Nuclear Roulette

"It was up to Petrov to confirm the incoming attack to his superiors, who would then launch a retaliatory strike while the missiles were still in the air. 'The chances it was real were 50-50', he recalled, 'But I didn't want to be the one responsible for starting a third world war.' So he told his commanders that the alarm was false. Much later, it emerged Soviet satellites had mistaken the sun's reflection in clouds for the start of a missile salvo." *Time,* October 2, 2017. "Stanislav Petrov, Cold War Hero," retired officer of the Soviet Air Defence Forces.

One man saved the world from holocaust in 1983. With this said, I introduce Nuclear Roulette in the humor tradition of Will Rogers: His earthy anecdotes and folksy style allowed him to poke fun at gangsters, prohibition, politicians, government programs, and a host of other controversial topics in a way that was appreciated by a national audience, with no one offended. His aphorisms, couched in humorous terms, were widely quoted: "I am not a member of an organized political party. I am a Democrat." Another widely quoted Will Rogers comment, "I don't make jokes. I just watch the government and report the facts."

The following is historically true, spiced with innocent satire and with more questions than answers. You decide.

History: 100 nuclear tests were conducted at the Nevada test site north of Las Vegas from 1951 through 1962. Unfortunately a rogue wind during a test spread radiation as far as Arizona, perhaps beyond.

Satire: Though now it's illegal to test nuclear atmospheric detonations in other countries, it's still legal in New Mexico and Nevada. Therefore our military Industrial Complex during our Cold War with Russia decided that the Nevadan outback was the right place to register an atmospheric nuclear mining claim. All this was done, of course, in light of our clear and present danger. It was an unusual mining claim; nevertheless, the military got its mining claim.

And since Nevada had neither a nuclear bomb deterrent nor a defense system with which to defend herself, she allowed the Consortium to nuke her outback atmosphere as long as it was designated a mining claim with the proper paperwork, accompanied by credible atmospheric samples.

Government scientists and the military promised that the atmospheric nuclear tests would not harm Reno nor Las Vegas wild life, nor patriotic voters. Already I sense trouble in River City.

A specific stipulation in the nuclear mining claim prohibited contaminated winds reaching population centers. Of course, this fail-safe testing depended on accurate weather reports. Not to worry, casino managers assured us that Lady Luck wouldn't let the wind get out of hand. She is married to the casinos, you know, and in the percentage and hope business. Nuclear testing must not make Lady Luck look bad. That would be bad for business.

Once more, Nevada insisted that the word nuclear atmosphere testing be digitally scrambled by legal-speak to be a harmless upper atmosphere mining claim. They had to keep those sneaky newspaper reporters away. Otherwise, if the truth was known—just a whisper would scare tourists away from Las Vegas and Reno's gaming slots, roulette wheels, dice and blackjack tables. The slightest rumor of nuclear danger would upset Lady Luck. She needs to be happy to make the gaming business work. Furthermore, Nevada can't let the Cold War interfere with state controlled Las Vegas-Reno gaming. She needs taxes. Nevada is not stupid. No siree.

Also, to make this atmospheric mining claim legal, the mining site had to be zoned wasteland with no real estate value. Furthermore the claim had to be posted miles away from buildings, clusters of animals, and people. Once again, it had to be conducted in such a way as to not to scare horses, stampede cattle, trouble sheep and wildlife, nor injure people. It was an unusual mining claim; nevertheless, the military got its mining rights.

Nevada did not idly stand by while nuclear folks nuked her upper atmosphere real estate. No siree! In the spirit of the Old West, Nevada collected enough tax money to build highways that her taxpaying citizens didn't have to pay for.

Thankfully, our guardian angel did not allow us to turn the Cold War into a radioactive hot war and turn our planet into a wasteland. Otherwise, instead of writing this satire at my desk, I would be drifting in atmospheric dust or hunkered down somewhere in a mountain cave eating stale WWII C rations.

Since the road to hell is paved with good intentions, and no good deed the government does goes without unforeseen consequences, during a nuclear test, a rogue wind carried radioactive fallout down-wind as far as Arizona—maybe further. Along the way, prairie dogs, sheep, wildlife and some people in my hometown of Camp Verde, Arizona still glow in the dark.

Oh well, ya gotta give the military-industrial complex and meteorologists a little patriotic slake now and then. How else could we have fought the Cold War without friendly fire?

Not to forget, our government folks do have hearts and do care for us. And not to forget, we do have the best government that money can buy. Consequently, for those who could prove that their cancers were caused by this nuclear fallout, each received $50,000, which helped cover medical and funeral expenses.

Written in 2017.

Monticello

Doris and I once visited Monticello, Thomas Jefferson's home in Virginia, and walked room to room and from garden to cemetery. We walked back over the hushed centuries to the painful birth of our country.

Of course, we know that Thomas Jefferson wrote the first draft of the Declaration of Independence.

This we also know, many in the thirteen colonies, Tories, remained loyal to England and King George and rejected the need for a revolutionary war with England. That's now history.

This great document has been read and listened to by more audiences than any other political document. To this day, well-worn phrases such as "self-evident truths" and "unalienable rights" have not lost their power to inspire people the world around.

At the time, flowing fresh from Jefferson's pen, the idealistic phrases of the Declaration of Independence were thought too unrealistic, too generous, and too dangerous, because they gave common people rights that traditionally belonged only to kings and rulings classes; nevertheless, our nation's founders valued their freedoms and knew that it could only be safeguarded within a democratic republic.

However, from the outset, Jefferson was no utopian idealist oblivious to the seven deadly sins and the rebellious nature of humanity. Therefore, he wisely balanced unalienable rights with self-evident truths. Rights and reason must always balance.

Also, the framers of our Constitution knew the clear and present danger of a theocracy; religion tends to corrupt the state and the state tends to corrupt religion. This new Constitution would provide a safe place for the state and religion to serve the common good.

Also, Thomas Jefferson knew that citizens would be tempted to champion personal rights at the expense of truth, justice, and the common good.

Richard Wentz: "Montesquieu long ago warned that the future of a republic depends on the future of virtue in its citizens."

Eugene Linden: "As human history has shown, once minds break free of religious, cultural and physical controls, they burn hot and fast, consuming and altering everything around them."

"Freedom, however, is not the last word. Freedom is only part of the story and half of the truth. Freedom is but the positive aspect of the whole phenomenon whose negative aspect is responsibleness. In fact, freedom is in danger of degenerating into mere arbitrariness unless it is lived in terms of responsibleness. That is why I recommend that the Statue of Liberty on the East Coast be supplemented by a Statue of Responsibility on the West Coast." Viktor Frankl, *Man's Search for Meaning*

Written in 1995.

America

I have always honored my country, obeyed her known laws, and served her in many ways. As a citizen, I and my country are one. I have visited and briefly lived in other counties. Though I enjoyed the people, their cultures, and their sights, I always looked forward to being home.

Our Declaration of Independence states:

When in the Course of human events, it becomes necessary for one people to dissolve the political bands which have connected them with another, and to assume among the powers of the earth, the separate and equal station to which the Laws of Nature and of Nature's God entitle them, a decent respect to the opinions of mankind requires that they should declare the causes which impel them to the separation.

We hold these truths to be self-evident, that all men are created equal, that they are endowed by their Creator with certain unalienable Rights, that among these are Life, Liberty and the pursuit of Happiness. That to secure these rights, Governments are instituted among Men deriving their powers from the consent of the governed.

Remember "Governments are instituted among Men deriving their powers from the consent of the governed." And also remember we are the heirs of our founders' times, as well as citizens of their future. Like them, we too face an unknown future that will be as challenging as theirs.

As a result of their faith and action, over two hundred years of freedom and self-government now has placed us a superpower on the world stage. With this power comes responsibility.

John in Okinawa

Our Republic is an ongoing experiment, always has been, always will be. We will never be without hard choices and consequences. Even though America has changed many times, our country has managed to stay young in spirit. I believe in inspired leadership and saving events, spiritual awakenings, and amazing transformations. Each new generation is a new opportunity to change for the better. I have not lost faith.

I believe that at the last trumpet this present historical curtain will fall. Then, the faithful will sing new songs and dream new dreams. Then they will look back and say to each other "It was worth it."

Written in 2015.

The Library

In 1962, the town's small, stone jail was retired and became an honored member of Camp Verde Arizona Historical Society. What stories this stone jail once heard? Perhaps future technologies will retrieve them from cold stone. But for now the old jail is just secret silence and small space.

In case you wonder where that small stone jail is, it's standing uptown across the street from the former Camp Verde Public School. Interestingly, after the town retired the stone jail in 1962, it became the town's first library. This is not to say the books in the jail library imprisoned the mind.

In 1965, my wife and I, plus two daughters and a son, moved to Camp Verde and we began a pastoral ministry—a social and spiritual catalyst most interesting and productive, more by virtue of my family, more than my own. This was before Camp Verde was incorporated, and before the original library building was built.

Through the years our library had grown from the patient dreams of many. What we now call the "old" library came into being after the "old jail" became too small in the 1970s.

Our new library is only an abstract sculpture, anybody's guess by those who haven't seen its architecture dimensions in virtual image (2015).

It's not just a large, expensive building; it will be a university of the best minds of the world—past, present, and future. Amazingly, no tuition required; the library will be free to all. (2016)

But for now, our new Library is just gray concrete and naked steel with workmen going about their business like a hive of bees building their multi-storied comb library for future bees, honey, and pollen.

When finished, our new Camp Verde Community Library will be two stories tall, even now crowding our old single-story library. When finished it will inherit all the property and the present library will become history's memory.

In November of 2016 our new Library's heart will beat, lights will turn on, plumbing will flush, computers will connect, and books will fill rows of shelves. This will be just its beginning.

What dreams may come?

A supporting sidebar of this story: As a VVMC volunteer chaplain, when I visit Maternity, I often see a newborn attended by nurse and aide. Since the baby had left its mother, it's now a visiting stranger in a strange new world the infant cannot possibly understand. The infant cannot know what has happened nor survive without help. Most likely, though, the baby senses separation from its mother and soon after senses others. We've all been there and done that. Now, the baby's personal journey begins through Life, consequently its personal library also begins. By the time the baby reaches childhood, it will have added thousands of memory books to its personal library, from which the baby makes sense of this strange and exciting world.

Just as important, the baby will learn who it is and how to relate to social settings. To accomplish this, the baby's social library will exponentially expand with books written by others.

In our fast-changing consequently challenging technological culture, when the baby becomes a child, at first it will be taught at home, then in our free public school system, which includes elementary school, followed by high school. We have found this to be the best way to teach the growing child how to become a responsible, informed, and contributing member of its community.

Our young adults may then choose college and university education, or mentoring programs; however, even there he/she will be taught by others (hopefully) more mature and educated, thus adding more books to their personal libraries.

Written in 2015. Revised in 2017.

On the Road with Kids

Picture a family of five on the road to Disneyland and every parent and kid knows what's going to happen along the way.

Safe behind safety belts and airbags, the car's radio lazily plays background music, interrupted occasionally by the announcer. The traffic is easy and it's not yet time for a pit stop. Mom is peacefully watching the world go by and dad is watching the road ahead. Parents are content. Kids are bored.

Three restless kids in the backseat, one boy four, one boy six, and one girl eight who ask, "Are we there yet?" After a dozen times, mom's happy vacation smile becomes a frown. She looks back for the umpteenth time and with a mommy-bear edge in her voice, says, "It's a long way yet, read the books you brought!" Clearly, the kids are not happy with mom's answer.

But kids quickly learn how to get parents to stop at filling stations for pee-time. It always works. Every parent who seriously studies kids knows that they are naturally born casino players, and every kid knows they must put something in the pot to stay in the game.

Dad turns off the interstate, finds a Chevron or Circle K gas station, and parks the car. The instant the car stops moving, the kids swing open doors and race to restrooms—parents close behind. Few moms will leave their kids alone with strangers in a public restroom.

After the restroom scam works, the kids dash for the pop and candy machines and longingly gaze at the treasures. Again, parents know what's happening; they once were kids, too. It's all theater, a game to be played on the family stage. Parents and kids play their parts—plead, frown, laugh, scold and smile a lot.

My suggestion is to always remember that an important part of a good vacation is to play this family game on the way. Also on the way to something more important, restroom scams and pop and candy machines will do, when the going gets long and dull.

Parents are grownup kids, and can always use pit-stops, timeouts and the exercise of keeping up with their kids. It's better than going to a gym and working out on exercise machines.

Finally, always read the books you brought when pit stops are far between.

Written in 2017.

Mexican Black Vultures

Mexican black vultures soared over Patagonia, Arizona today. They flew the evening sky of monsoon clouds, high up in a circle among themselves. These vultures flew in a three-dimensional square dance to the call and music of the Unseen One.

They flew in choreographed weaving, spiraling do-si-do, drawing close, drifting away. So close that I saw the sky between their feathers, so far up I saw them as dancing dots.

Gravity stuck me to this hill, glued me to earth as firm as rock. I stood among framing trees. A cool wind was in my face, but no wings to soar and no lifting power—so I thought.

Then my mind lifted up to the flying vultures. I felt thermals beneath my wings, saw the earth below, and saw myself a speck looking up. Such is the gift of imagination. Feathers whispered and I knew the freedom of flight.

One bird left the dance and as if by secret signal flew west into the fading summer storm. It flew toward Nogales until it was but a black speck against an orange sunset behind scrim of clouds. The speck dissolved. Others followed.

I had become the illusion my mind had chosen to believe; but now my illusion had faded into reality. I'm back to where I never left. Such is the gift of imagination.

Written in 1996.

Over Mingus Mountain

My Mingus Mountain story paints a word picture of a lone cyclist, a child-like deer, and a crazy mixed-up squirrel.

I drove over Arizona' Mingus Mountain last week and on the way I met a lone cyclist struggling up the switchbacks. She was heavy with pannier saddlebags, which made her lonely struggle all the more desperate. She seemed to be as vulnerable as a deer. I wanted to stop and chat with her about our common interest in cycling, but on second thought—sometimes wisdom works for me—I feared she would take my good will to be a stranger's unwanted attention. I smiled, waved, and prayed for her safety, then left her alone to enjoy her Mingus bike ride. Having done it, it's like climbing a long staircase into forever. And if you can do it in middle chain-ring pedal by pedal for an hour or so, you will eventually reach the top and spin down the other side.

Driving over Mingus Mountain was an ice cream sundae in May. On this narrow, winding road from Jerome to Prescott, the sun was warm and dazzling bright. The air was sweet and gentle as baby breath on my cheek.

Old snow and ice was on the shadow side of Mingus; snow too deep for deer. However, on the sun-side the snow sparkled like sprinklings of powdered sugar on chocolate cake. Around a bend, up ahead, five deer stood in the road. I cautiously approached. When they saw me, they turned in surprise, startled as children caught doing something naughty. Although I'm sure they heard me coming, they still registered that wild animal surprise when I came into view.

Perhaps they wondered if I was going to be a hungry predator, or only something harmless just passing through. I presume deer think like that. Deer gamble like that. As Canadian caribou have learned to live with wolves, our deer on Mingus have learned to live with lions, hunters, and cars and do not immediately run. Why waste good energy in needless flight if what they hear and see is not hungry. Most prey animals know hunger when they smell and see it.

A Mingus Mountain squirrel ran into the road just ahead of me, but at the last moment changed its mind, did a summersault, and dashed back for cover. Though cunning in many ways, squirrels become absolutely stupid when involved with cars—like some people I know.

Strangely, squirrels at times seem suicidal in their poor judgment and poor timing. I've had them run from perfect safety right into my wheels. When that happens, it's sad to see. It's not right for such a splendid animal to come to its end as a soft bump under a hard tire. Nailed in the talons of a hawk, the end of a hungry bobcat's chase or a fast food snack for wily coyote makes more sense—yes, but to dash into the path of a car when safety lies merely in doing nothing is so useless. Obviously, generations of experience with road machines has not had time to download this danger in their tiny craniums. A small consolation but a redeeming truth in the economy of nature: nothing is wasted. The dead squirrel may soon soar the mountain skies in the talons of a hawk, or in the belly of a raven, or live again in the form of a fox. There are no morticians in nature, only appetites.

Born in nature's cradle, wildlife soon learns the house rules: adapt, migrate, or die. Harsh as it sounds, it's clean and sure. It's a gambler's life which is anything but dull. To know when to hold and when to fold, to know when to hide and when to run, to stay or migrate, are the dues paid for the ride. Lessons quickly learned in wildlife's ever changing roulette wheel.

Jack London inked his pen with wild courage and wrote *The Call of the Wild*, while Walt Disney gave us animated animals with human intelligences and emotions. I ink my pen in Jack London's wild world.

Written in 2015.

Blueberry Hill

There's a place in the Ozarks, in the Beaver Lake area, that's just right for growing blueberries. The rainfall, humidity, temperature, and rich soil make blueberries a profitable business.

These berries ripen at least five weeks before New Jersey berries hit the market, and in the berry business first is best.

Doris and I visited a commercial blueberry farm (bush?) while on vacation in Arkansas. While there we visited Peter and Letty Hofstra—friends who once lived near us in Camp Verde, Arizona. They treated us to a hillbilly musical and mountain comedy show and a guided tour of a blueberry farm. Neat rows of mulched and trimmed berry bushes were signs of a successful business.

The family uses an automatic drip irrigation system that assures the right amount of water at the right time and relieves dependence on rain. They also apply the right sequences of spray that includes herbicides, insecticides, and a bird repellent. A root rot treatment is on standby for the first signs of that dreaded disease.

During the busy harvest, berries are picked by local folks, all eager to earn quick cash over the harvest season.

Of course, flocks of hungry birds like blueberries. But blueberry farmers and birds must get along for the business and the ecosystem to work. I say birds have the best part of this arrangement. They enjoy eating insects and worms that damage crops, and of course consume wild berries in season. The farmer's part is to find a way to protect his crops from birds without killing them. Bird spray seems, at least for now, to be an equitable compromise that in the long run works in the best interest of both parties.

Depending on the person telling the bird repellent story, the bird eats a sprayed blueberry and is unable to swallow it for few hours. This discourages pesky birds from coming back. It's a small price to pay for saving a crop and discouraging birds. The bottom line is blueberry growers stay in business and birds enjoy free lunches of insects, and blueberries when the spray doesn't work.

Here's a page from Nature's repellant playbook: A skunk's biodegradable spray will repel a grizzly bear, and the common toad has an irritating secretion embedded in its skin which will discourage all but the most naïve predator.

A fast memory rewind: We didn't have bird repellent to guard our cherries and berries on our farm in Michigan; instead, we hung black cutouts of owls in the trees. They did little more than advertise the fruit. Come and get it, the fruit is ripe.

To defend our cherries and berries, I hid in bushes and shot marauding birds with a BB gun, to this day with a bad conscious, but at that time it was more fun than guilt. In spite of my bird kills, cherry and berry loses remained about the same, with or without my BB gun. The reason for this was my bottomless appetite.

While on guard duty, compared to the birds, cherry by cherry, berry by berry, I managed to eat more than what the birds would have eaten. Now, I know that my grandmother would have come out ahead of my cherry-berry game if she had kept me away from the trees and bushes and let the birds have their way. But then, there was sly wisdom in her methods. I was a growing boy and three meals at her table needed supplementation by foraging the fruit of the land.

While we are on the bird and berry subject, I need to share the story of a Navajo who after failing to stop crows from digging up and eating his corn seed, invented an ingenious plan to outwit these feathered thieves. For several days in a row he merely pretended to plant his corn; consequently, each time the crows came they found nothing.

After several unrewarded trips to his field, the crows gave up and left. Then the farmer planted his seed corn. It worked for him.

Written in 1992.

Empty Places and Spaces

"Yet beneath his hands the clay visibly relaxes, finds that one still point and spins with the smooth grace of a ballerina, on center." *The Road Through Miyama* by Leila Philip

A potter begins with handfuls of clean clay plumped on his potter's wheel. The spinning wheel's centrifugal energy enters the clay, which in turn prepares it to yield to the potter's intended design. His hands begin to form its emptiness. It may be a common bowl, an expensive work of art, a flower vase, or a tempered prayer bell.

Behavioral scientists know by experiment that a monitored volunteer isolated in an empty, soundproof room will in time lose his grip on reality and form an illusionary inner world. This is not the emptiness of this essay.

This common story may seem strange to a Christian but not to a Buddhist: Once a novice Buddhist monk asked his master, "What is Buddhism?" After a respectful time, the Master gave the young monk this *koan* (puzzle): "Go wash your begging bowl." The young monk was surprised; though this simple answer seemed strange, he knew his master was serious and wise. While washing his begging bowl he thought about the *koan*. Failing to understand, he set the bowl aside and went about his duties. The next morning the monks from the monastery visited the village market with their begging bowls. The merchants supported the monks by placing vegetables, fruit and grains in their bowls. Christians have offering plates; Buddhist monks have begging bowls.

Suddenly, the young monk knew the answer to his *koan*: Buddhism is personal emptiness. Monks keep their inner lives washed of yesterday in order to receive what will be today. They live one day at a time.

Christians practice emptiness when they pray The Lord's Prayer which includes "Give us this day our daily bread," and the petition: "forgive us our trespasses as we forgive those who trespass again us." This prayer includes our dependence on others for food and forgiveness.

We all live by our emptiness and one day at a time. Our bowls are filled each day by others. For instance, people push shopping carts in grocery stores, drifting up and down aisles and fill their carts with what is produced by others.

Vehicles are produced by others. Children are nurtured by parents and teachers. Police protect, militaries defend, and the medical community serves the well and sick. No one is an island. For this to take place each works according to their ability and each receives according to their need. It's called justice and civilization.

When an empty cathedral bell calls people to worship and time of day, its sound is heard for miles.

Empty spaces in courtrooms allow truth to be searched and found in law, witness, and facts.

When the flutist exhales her breath into a flute and her fingers select notes, the hollow in the flute sings.

Empty places in conversations allow others to smoothly enter without interruptions or collision of words.

Empty places in traffic maintain safe spaces between vehicles. By law and courtesy, no tailgating, no crowding, no double-line passing.

While bicycling, I maintained a buffer zone, an empty space between me and vehicles.

A healthy nation sets aside empty places and spaces for rest and healing, for dreams and visions.

The empty space between trees in a forest gives each tree light and freedom to grow

In Nature there are empty places and spaces for peace and wonder, loneliness for some, holiness for others.

We cannot be civilized without spaces and places.

Written in 2007.

What If

A Parable: What if the world and every TV screen suddenly went blank-white—nothing for five days, while technicians worked to find the cause.

Five days later, the universe appeared on each screen. Star clusters gleamed against black velvet space, galaxies spiraled, and the Milky Way was a sparkling necklace of night-lights.

Again, five days later our solar system zoomed in and our emerald earth filled the screen. Absolute Silence.

The U.S. blamed terrorists, Iran blamed Israel, and the science community believed a computer virus had infected communication satellites.

Then after another five days, a human form electronically developed on screens and reflected in the pools of human minds.

Then, after five more days each heard in their own language: "I am your Creator God, The Big ONE."

Each person perceived the Deity according to their belief system. Some panicked and turned off their TVs, and retreated into denial. Some drifted into shock; others dismissed it as an advertising trick. A few believed it to be the antichrist and others worshipped their TV sets. Most wanted to believe. After five more days the human form spoke again:

I gave you the gift of flesh and free will including imagination. With these gifts above other creatures anything you imagine can happen. You are free to form heaven or hell on earth.

I spoke to Moses in a burning bush, I sent prophets of truth and I became Spirit-filled flesh in Jesus of Nazareth. Also I hid in plain sight in nature and spoke in conscience and whispers in hearts of people of good will. Even so, most did not take Me seriously. What's worse, many explained me away and traded me for secularism, nihilism, and atheism.

Now, I come to you in non-religious technology. I know your skepticism; therefore, I will reveal myself in the universal language of Nature and science. Next Monday, a small earthquake will tremble the San Francisco Peaks; the following Tuesday, a five-day rain will fall on sub-Sahara Africa, and the day after the Jordan River will flow backwards.

Fear not, I will not take back your gifts; however, I will restrict them until you grow up and become a mature people. Until then, I will hold in trust other gifts you cannot imagine. In the meantime, I will not allow you to destroy yourselves nor the earth through your fear, pride, greed, and ignorance. My angels will enforce this edict.

Now comes the hard part: from this day forward the Earth is a peace zone. You must destroy your weapons and learn war no more. Furthermore, I now forbid Western nations to treat the Middle East as a big, dumb, gas station, and I forbid Islamic militants to terrorize the World. My angels will enforce this also.

This is really going to hurt: I gave you religion as a mirror that would reflect my thoughts, but too often you invented your own mirrors that reflect your own thoughts, imaginations, doctrines, and superstitions. Consequently, I am now your religion. I will be your All in All. I will lead you in the paths of righteousness for my name's sake. To *make this happen, each Holy Day I will enter your TVs and teach you face to face.*

Until we meet again, my advice to you is lighten-up and get a life. I now return control of your TVs back to you.

The Almighty, The Big One, God,
Shalom.
P.S. I love you

A version of "What If" was published as "The Voice" in the *Verde View on* October 31, 1978.

Senior Christians

Senior Christians are God's fall flowers, with less time to bloom again, but no less valued in the sight of God. Everyone will become a senior if they live long enough.

Each senior knows life is far too short and winter much too soon. But still, each one in heart, no less in seed, patiently waits for life's rebirth.

Until then, capable seniors, rich in experience, wisdom, and disposable incomes serve as examples and guides for youth's listening ears. That is, if the senior is still young in heart.

Keep in mind, the senior population is not an obsolete life form; it's a vibrant, renewable resource. A surprise for some middle-agers are becoming seniors in higher numbers than the U.S. birth rate. Even as I write, the leading edge of the Baby Boomer generation is slipping into seniority and, if not hopelessly delusional, they will discover or rediscover their mortality and seek spiritual guidance. Guess what? Show Time, Big Time, for the church.

The first obstacle a Baby Boomer meets is a "forever-young" illusion generated by our pop culture. No grumpy or grumpier old men, no hearing loss, no creaky joints, and no diseases are allowed in this magical kingdom of make-believe. This in turn conditions youth to believe seniors inhabit a mythical far-far-away kingdom of hospitals, nursing homes, endless RV vacations with spoiled poodles, and mindless TV. This, too, is an illusion promoted by the entertainment and advertising media. Also it encourages ageism and marginalization. For this reason, it's not helpful for a church to embrace this pop culture.

Many sincere Christians believe that their church must attract young adults and children or their church will weaken and die. In other words, if a church has only seniors, it's on the skids. These are discouraging words for seniors. First spoken, this anointed incantation sounds like "The whole truth and nothing but the truth, so help me God." However, after reasonable reflection, I'm convinced it is only an illusion. Though I do believe we are to seek, greet and love all without prejudice, I also believe that demographic balances in churches widely vary over time and years. Some have more youth than seniors; others have more seniors. Even so, these churches do live and thrive. If in God's providence, a church becomes a senior congregation, it still can be a dynamic church. It's built into the system. Prayer and qualified ministries can be effective.

In conclusion, this I believe to be true: most seniors I know are smart and active, and will not be marginalized nor stereotyped, nor will they attend a church for long if it does not seriously address their existential questions, nor satisfy their hunger for deep spirituality and their longing for belonging.

Furthermore, seniors are quick to notice a favoring of a shallow pop culture to the exclusion of a deep Christian spirituality.

What if God calls a church to add a senior ministry and that church is not listening?

Written in 2005.

The Marriage Candle

Rainer Maria Rilke understood how challenging marriage can be: "For one person to love another, this is the most difficult of all our tasks."

I write only of Christian Marriage. The photo of the marriage candle with the flame sheltered by my hands was taken immediately after a church wedding ceremony I solemnized. Rings were exchanged, two became one, and the one became greater than the sum of the two. Faith, hope, and love energize the union. It was then legalized at my desk by signatures of bride and groom, two witnesses, and the minister, me.

Christian marriage is commitment and vows sanctified in the presence of God and witnesses for a new way of living for a man, a woman, and their children. The couple trades singleness for togetherness with the possibility of bringing new life into this world.

Marriage is needful for a healthy family life, providing a refuge for father, mother, and their children as it adapts to life's necessary challenges and changes, as well as a foundation for community. For this marriage to be successful, the bride and groom must become one in the other through respect and love for each other. That makes it a fast track to mental and spiritual maturity.

Teaching Time
Aubrey (granddaughter), Doris (grandmother),
Joanna (great-grandmother) and newborn Baby Oliver.
Trisha (mother, not shown)

There are no perfect marriages, only successful ones. Living a marriage by flawed and mistake-making people is not without struggle and high costs over time. It requires unusual commitment to the union. If one member fails, both suffer, the children suffer, and their community suffers, too. If the candle flame flutters in that ill-wind and becomes a spark and the wick is not relit, the marriage dies.

A true story: After a difficult divorce a little girl's father left. One day, the mother peeked into her daughter's room and saw her sitting before the photo of her father. In tears the little girl said, "I will be good, please come back."

As a volunteer chaplain at our local hospital, while making my rounds, I visited a couple in their nineties. They had been married 75 years, but still were young in heart. Though their marriage candle had burned nearly to its end, it still flamed. Once more, the couple still had that new bride and groom look of love for each other.

Written in 2013.

Old Catholic Churches

Now and then I enjoy visiting time-honored (old) Catholic churches, like the one in Jerome, Arizona. When I do, I'm aware of architecture, space, design, and sunlight filtering through stained glass windows.

I study steps leading to the chancel and the proper rows of pews, like old soldiers inviting worshippers to sit. I smell the polished floors and pews and the wax prayer candles, sometimes beeswax candles, too. I know faithful people still care and keep the church alive.

Though now without bees, I am still a beekeeper and easily recognized the scent of old beeswax candles. It's embedded in the wood. I know because I'm a beekeeper, a bee charmer, a self-ordained priest of Nature, and a minister of the protestant Church. I don't protest.

In former times before the church turned to paraffin candles, churches used beeswax candles. As they burned their earthy fragrance was embedded in woodwork, and in the hearts and memories of worshippers.

There is a metaphorical meaning of beeswax in Christian tradition. Virgin house bees produce beeswax, with which they form beeswax comb. Therefore, when the church burns beeswax candles in worship, the candles become reminders of the Virgin Mary.

This I believe, The Godhead is a singularity of transcendence and immanence. This I also believe: religions need the holy male and female in their traditions and in their doctrinal core to be fully human, fully spiritual, fully peaceful, and good neighbors to others.

I must say, when I'm resting in this spiritual dimension a world away from our busy world just outside, while in the presence of stained glass windows and unlocked door, I am in peace and creative thought flows like springs of living water. All this reminds me of my pastoral appointments, not without a tear or two.

My other world too often forgets the power of sacred spaces and places.

Written in 2014.

Alan Sees God

Once upon a time in the land of make-believe a wealthy young man, Alan Smith, lived among us. He was a graduate of an Ivy League university, a member of a politically powerful family, the young CEO of a successful company, and was well connected in political and social circles.

What's more, Alan owned a mountain retreat, a private jet, and a yacht. More importantly, Alan enjoyed excellent health, was well married to his faithful young wife, Ruth, and all their children were above average.

And because his successes had come easily, Alan had not learned to be thankful. He was likeable, congenial, and generous, but pathetically spoiled in a nice sort of way. His wife and friends told him so, but Alan only laughed. He had always achieved what he wanted and was denied nothing he set his heart on. Consequently Alan believed it all came due to his superior intelligence and efforts.

Of course, Alan had his bucket list of which all had been crossed off long ago, except one: Alan wanted to see God, The Almighty, The Big One. That one event on his list had been denied him, and it made him unhappy.

Finally, Alan decided to seek the help of his saintly minister, who listened to the young man's problem, then warned him that no man can actually see The Almighty—and live.

His good minister then quoted a Talmudic rabbi: "If not visible, The Almighty was accessible. Although humans cannot comprehend his ultimate essence, they may observe manifestations of His divine activity in creation and in the dynamics of history and society."

Then again, some believe God hides in plain sight.

Finally, his minister asked Alan what he thought God looked like. Alan answered, "Sometimes I think God is a brilliant point of light, or thunder and lightning in a giant cloud, or a voice from a burning bush not consumed. Maybe hearing is the same as seeing. Maybe God was an experience of an interstellar journey millions of light years in seconds, with an encore of birth and death of stars."

His minister smiled. The Almighty smiled. They both knew Alan had created God in his own image.

Alan's minister advised patience. "Don't worry, everyone will see The Almighty when they die." This didn't sit well with Alan who replied, "I want to see God now. I may live another 50 years. I can't wait that long." His minister sighed. "Alan, I can't help you with this."

Most people the minister counseled had ordinary problems that could be fixed. Nevertheless, since he was a kind minister and not wanting to dismiss Alan out of hand, he warned him that seeing The Almighty was not a safe seat in a theater, nor a thrill ride in a Disney theme park. It would be a life-changing experience. The good minister knew his impatient parishioner would see The Almighty in the way he needed, not in the way he wanted.

With that said, the minister withdrew to his office and laid Alan's request before The Almighty, with whom he was on good terms. He patiently waited for an answer. In his heart he hoped The Almighty would just say no, and that would end the matter, or He would just ignore the request with silence. Silence works for The Almighty.

After an hour of waiting one doesn't presume upon nor rush the Big One. The minister emerged from his office, looked Alan in the eyes and told him God said "Tell Alan, What! You can't wait five months?"

Alan is no longer unhappy. He is terrified, broken, and confused. Religion was not working for him. Even faith, hope and love faded into empty words. God hadn't given him what he wanted; God had given him a nightmare.

Alan returned home, hugged and kissed his wife, and told her what he had learned. He then began to make final arrangements. Although Alan had lost all meaning in life and was suffering clinical depression, he thought of his wife and children and wrote his will. Then Alan descended into a deep sleep. Alan's timeless journey began.

As orbiting Hubble reflects galaxies in its mirror and then digitizes them in photos, Alan saw the transcendent glories of God reflected in the mirror of his mind. Epiphanies followed. Alan saw angels, good and evil, and heaven and hell as states of mind. Alan knew he could never be mortal again and live in human society. The Almighty smiled.

Alan's dream-time continued. He became earth, flora and fauna. He saw himself as an animal becoming a spark of holy fire and Adam becoming a living soul. He saw himself a zygote, an embryo, a baby born. He became his father and mother. He became his wife and children, and his friends. Alan saw his wealth and possessions as meaningless trophies.

A stranger embraced his wife. His family drifted. His friends drifted, too. His business became another's. He walked to his cemetery and read his tombstone, and watched his life fade into oblivion.

When Alan's dream-time neared its calendared end and his clock ticked time to go, he awoke from his cocooning dream, gathered his family and friends and waited for his death moment. It was a miserable time for all. His deadline drew near. All held their breaths. Time stood still, time began again. Surprise, Alan was alive. All clapped for joy and thankfulness. His old self had passed away; he had become a new man, a very happy new man.

Alan hugged and kissed his children, then embraced his wife and kissed her again and again. The Almighty smiled.

Written in 2016.

Heaven and Hell

A Christian couple died and went to Wal-Mart. The greeter at the front door smiled and said, "Here's a gift card for a million earth-dollars, spend it freely, there's more where this comes from."

Well, the delighted couple had a wonderful time shopping. Several shopping carts later they checked out and left for the front door and parking lot. The greeter stopped them and said, "You can't take anything out." Surprised and disappointed, nevertheless, they planned to come back the next day and shop.

After several weeks of this, it became clear that this was pointless and boring, and not what they had expected of heaven. So, they complained to the greeter. The greeter smiled and said, "Hell is supposed to be pointless and boring."

The test: The couple asked the greeter if there was something better, and the greeter smiled and said, "Yes, come on up."

Written in 2017.

Our Robot

Why are we interested in robots?

In Jewish folklore, a golem is an animated anthropomorphic being, magically created entirely from inanimate matter. There are many tales differing on how the golem was brought to life and afterward controlled.

The most famous golem narrative involves Judah Loew Bezalel, the late 16th century rabbi of Prague.

In the early 20th century a golem novel was written and a movie was produced. The cautionary tale of the movie *Frankenstein* shows what can happen when a man becomes a demigod. As the story unfolds, Dr. Frankenstein brings a cadaver back to life by surgery and lightning; inadvertently creating a human monster. Events did not turn out well for the contrite doctor when his monster escaped and a frightened mob with pitchforks and torches searched for it.

Another cautionary tale: In Stanley Kubrick's science fiction classic *2001: A Space Odyssey* an artificial intelligent (AI) robot, Hal, becomes paranoid and kills the space ship's astronauts, except one who survives and disables Hal.

Now we have the science fiction movie, *Ex Machina*, about an AI robot, Ava, who manages to outwit her creator. This movie raises important questions. Would future AI robots have human-like free will, conscience, compassion, love, joy and peace? Would they be capable of intuition and moral judgment? Would these robots voluntarily pray, worship, explore, and create original works of art and literature, thus acting in ways that traditionally have defined humanity? If so, would they no longer be robots? A worthy question: Would perfect AI robots form a perfect society which may lead to confinement or recycling of imperfect humans?

Our personal robot: the human soul is a gift of God that dwells in our robot bodies, a belief shared in different ways by all major religions.

In its beginning our robot bodies grew from DNA and earth's clay formed on the spinning wheel of time under the guiding hands of divinity, then tempered and tested in real time by nature's stern disciplines. Call this natural evolution or theistic evolution, the result is the same. This must follow: when our souls enter this world and began their journeys of allotted time, each has a personal human robot growing in their mother's wombs, male or female, capable of passing on their genetic codes by means of reproduction.

Furthermore, I believe each personal robot is an intelligent human animal with sensor nerve-circuits, internal organs, amazing learning potential, and extraordinary motor capabilities. Its energy source can be vegetarian, carnivore, or both. It can live off the land. Its digestive system converts food into useable energy. If we feed it something dangerous, it will expel it to save its life. Also, its waste is biodegradable. Furthermore, it comes with renewable and self-healing capabilities.

Our personal robot comes with multi-gigabits of memory. It is capable of learning exponentially and will obey our will without question. It is programmed to survive 24/7 and repairs itself while we nap and sleep.

Although it is programmed to obey our wills even though we do something harmful, it will warn us by fear. However, in emergencies, our personal robot's survival can be overwritten. Even if we are wrong, it will remain our faithful servant.

It only asks that we treat it wisely, give it time to rest, feed it well, and give it exercise. Barring accident and disease it should last to the completion of our journey. In addition, if its functions are properly programmed and not critically injured, it will always be our best friend. We will never be alone.

Finally, while nearing its natural end, it will continue to serve us with its last breath.

Written in 2017.

The Mysterious

Why are we drawn to mystery, the edge of life and death, and to danger real or imagined?

Why do we watch others risk life and limb in risky sports, mountain climbing, white water canoeing, and bungee jumping?

Why do we enjoy adventure myths and strange utopias in soft theater seats while munching fresh popcorn?

Why do we hunger for imagined worlds in novels of mystery, romance, dangerous universes, or science gone wrong?

Theologians and scientists search for the mystery before the Big Bang. Although theology and science have different definitions and explanations, both address the same questions: why the universe, why life, and what is the meaning of life. Though, if one is addicted to the search for The Almighty, he may miss the experience of just plain living, which is our primary responsibility.

Most live life as they know it and let other folks more qualified search for the Almighty. Most settle for a good job, a good roast beef sandwich, a salad, a hot dog, pumpkin and cherry pie, and a movie. Also, an evening with a loved one enjoying a chef's menu in an upscale restaurant is more satisfying then a search for the meaning of life.

Some folks devote their lives to fast cars and nice homes flipped often, which can be mysterious and life-changing, too. For those who passively stand and wait, there are many mysterious twists and turns in life, though not as thrilling as a mountain climb up a sheer rock wall.

Others are drawn to the imagined horrors of Frankenstein, Werewolf, and Dracula. These are durable horror template themes that keep popping up, each time with more sophistication and better special effects.

Star Wars is a serial thriller. Not to forget *2001: A Space Odyssey* and *2010: The Year We Made Contact.* In the movie *Independence Day* we were invaded by weird aliens who demanded our surrender and go gentle into our last good night.

The Exorcist and *The Omen* plumbed the depth of demonic evil, while *Jaws* and its sequels exploit our primal fear of being eaten alive.

Then we have *Jurassic Park* to add to our library of human greed and nature out of control. *Jurassic Park* is good science fiction. The ethics and language are decent. One may even glean some paleontology and biotechnology information from the story.

This story begins with dinosaurs grown from DNA salvaged from dinosaur blood siphoned by ancient mosquitoes entombed in amber. A sudden thought: It's best to keep dinosaurs where they were.

A greedy computer programmer temporarily shuts down the electric dinosaur containment system to give himself time to meet a buyer of stolen dinosaur embryos. He takes a wrong turn and meets his demise in the jaws of small, hungry dinosaurs.

Of course, shutting down the theme park's computer, which keeps dinosaurs where they are supposed to be, starts the adrenaline of the story. For a good story, we must have a protagonist and antagonist, and all the players between. This one has them all. Once again we are reminded that human nature guarantees failure, and that there are no fail-safe systems, only backup fail-safe systems.

"Seek Immediate Shelter. This is not a drill." the false ballistic missile alert to Hawaii on January 13, 2018 took 38 minutes before the all clear. It was an edge of life and death experience. Why do we do this to ourselves?

My thoughts: The greatest mystery is God. If all the sand of all beaches and deserts of the world is a metaphor for the knowledge of God, what we now know and understand is only one grain of sand, with more deserts and beaches to come. For us there is no final frontier. There is no final mystery. God is here, everywhere, in every experience, and infinitely beyond. We have just begun.

Written in 2018.

The Current Beneath

One sunny day I was snorkeling off a California beach and Doris was relaxed and watching. I had ventured about fifty yards out into deep water when I felt a strong undertow pushing me south, parallel to the beach. I couldn't swim against it, so I swam with the undertow at an angle that took me back to shore. Scary, but it ended well. I walked back to where Doris watched. She was relieved to see me; she had lost sight of me and feared the worst.

Since she was near her time to deliver our son John, her fear for me had started her birth countdown. We drove through heavy Saturday traffic to our Mesa hospital where her doctor was called just in time to deliver our son. Though a close call, it was a happy time. We were both young and laughed it off.

There is a story in common domain about two aliens sent to earth to study humans. While hovering in a tiny space craft over a baseball game they studied competing teams hit a ball with a stick then run to safe bases. Someone threw the ball and someone caught it in a leather glove. A human in black directed the game with body language and words like safe, strike, foul, and out. Spectators stood up and waved their arms and yelled when some action in the field excited them.

These aliens knew not the logic of the action below because they knew not the rule book, human culture, and its invisible sportsmanship ethic in the current below and within.

I subscribe to the *Outdoor Photographer Magazine* and read the September 2017 article "The Big Picture, Life Force" by Amy Gulick. She writes well of her experience of visiting the McNeil River State Game Sanctuary in Alaska and its annual salmon run. She shared a photo of a brown bear catching a salmon. As the bear clamped his grip on the female salmon, she released loose beads of pink salmon eggs. The salmon became food for the bear's survival, but death for the salmon and her future.

Truly, life in this world is one big banquet at which predator and prey sit together. Here, there are no bystanders, only winners and losers, births and deaths, renewals and changes. All are just actors on the stage of life following scripts written by their ancestors in their books of changes. All must adapt, migrate or pass into oblivion. Nothing personal, just rules of the game written by the Creator of Life. All must change in the current beneath and within, which we call evolution. Ah, that Darwinian heavy word that often places science and religion in opposite corners. Coming to mind just now: Indigenous people have a saying: "If birds used words, they couldn't fly."

Merriam-Webster's Collegiate Dictionary: "Darwinism: In 1864 Charles Darwin published a theory of the origin and perpetuation of new species of animals and plants that offspring of a given organism vary, that natural selection favors the survival of some of these variations over others, that new species have arisen and may continue to rise by these processes, and that widely divergent groups of plants and animals have risen from the same ancestors."

When Charles Darwin studied animal and plant life on the Galapagos Islands off Ecuador and published his theory in *Origin of Species*, many people of faith accepted his theory of evolution as the spiritual current beneath and within

Biblical Genesis' figurative poetry, while others of faith continued to believe a literal interpretation.

By the way, Darwin has been described as one of the most influential figures in human history and is honored by burial in Westminster Abbey.

A poet's thought: "The upward rise of natural clay on evolution's potter wheel of change and time, and the pruning of predator and prey explains how life interacts from the beginning to this day." Perhaps God is like a Genesis gardener or farmer planting seeds and cultivating what grows.

In the Middle Ages, cathedrals were built in the center of European cities and did not instantaneously become cathedrals. These buildings of worship slowly rose from foundation stone by stone, and wood by wood, by glass and by human hand.

The soft war between Biblical literalism and theistic evolution, not pantheism but pan-en-theism, continues. Though it's not as passionate as it once was.

I keep in mind that every belief system and its practice such as medicine, psychology, astronomy, mathematics, physics, social formations, economics, and moderate religions have changed and will continue to change with discovery. Humanity is far from finished in its search for truth. Therefore, it's wise to be humble and to have a deep running hunger and thirst for truth wherever it's found. It's also good to be willing to say "Whoops, I was wrong."

Final thought: When an innocent child sees a bee in a flower gathering pollen and sipping nectar, the child knows only the simple wonder of a bee in a flower.

Written in 2017.

Dante's View

The poet, Dante, wrote of his exile and wandering: "A bark without sail and without rudder, borne to diverse ports and bays and shores by that dry wind which grievous poverty breathes forth."

Dante's View in California's Death Valley National Park gave us a vulture's view of the Badwater Basin salt flats and the hot heart of Death Valley.

Instead of wandering by ship without sail and rudder on a rolling sea, we traveled in the safety of two all-terrain vehicles on a sea of sand in the shaggy places of Arizona, California, and Wyoming. We visited and photographed ghost towns and abandoned gold mines and camped under the stars wherever evening found us.

Sometimes we traveled along narrow wagon trails that snaked up and down dry washes and through miles of cacti and forests of Joshua trees. At other times we struggled up and down narrow mountain roads, cut in haste from steep mountainsides strewn with meteor belts of rocks—goat trails I called them. Blind curves and drop-offs without guard rails sucked breath and raced the heart.

Rooster tail combs of quartz were good signs of gold below. They were starting places for many mines. Wandering prospectors dug by pick and shovel vertical exploratory shafts and followed the gold-bearing quartz down until they either ran out of promise or opened veins of gold. Many old shafts were unfenced poverty holes waiting to catch men and animals unaware. Most held rattlesnake nests.

Outside of Shoshone a dirt road separated from blacktop and led us through Death Valley on our way to the ghost town of Greenwater, California. Quail had squatters' rights in this haunted place. A sign marked the community where hundreds of people once lived, dreamed, and finally yielded to an exhausted gold mine and financial ruin. Rusted barrel hoops, old cars and parts, and five-gallon water cans huddle near the sign as if to find a center for their loneliness. Ore dumps and mine tailings led the eye to mine entrances, now slim pickings for rock hound scavengers. Again, they told stories of faded hopes and bankrupt dreams.

A covey of quail scattered at our approach to an open mine shaft, then called to each other from the sage and brittle bush. The quail were the only signs of moving life in this burned out place.

I listened carefully for sounds in the wind. Faintly, I heard women and children laughing and men going about the business of a mining camp. How much suggested by the Greenwater sign? How much suggested by collections of rusted junk and open mine shafts? How much suggested from history and myths of Western movies? And how much suggested by active imagination? I couldn't say.

We drove one hundred and sixty-five miles over a crushed salt and sand road to Furnace Creek, then south to Dagget. Just think of the terrible thirst of man and mules trudging over a road built by sledge hammering a crust of salt and sand into a wagon trail. If one listens, one can hear, from long ago, the hoarse yells of muleskinners driving twenty-mule-team borax wagons.

From Dante's View we traveled east through a mountain range and camped that night on a ridge. The next morning we descended the west side into Joshua trees and yucca cacti and traveled in and out of washes through the driest land in the Southwest.

We came upon an abandoned ranch house and half expected to see Shoshone arrows sticking out of sidings and defenders lying inside among rifle cartridges. But this was 1982, not 1872. A rusted truck, assorted tools, and a beat-up air compressor marked the time. We needed that reference. The solitude was like that of Greenwater—a world without people, like the day after the end of the world.

In the yard, children's toys lay about just as the children left them in their last play, and in the house debris was scattered over the floor, along with a hint of ammonia—pack rat urine. Old magazines and yellowed newspapers printed the day and date. Odds and ends of pots, pans, dishes, and kitchen utensils were dropped from where they were last used, unwashed. We pulled open drawers of an old dressers and saw that pack rats had moved in and built nests.

Who were they who left without taking things and cleaning? Nothing of value remained, only dust, dirt, and debris of careless living and hasty leaving.

Perhaps the last human tenants were vacationing counterculture flower children who visited this house in the 1960s and 70s to chill out, communicate with nature, and alter their minds with recreational drugs. Or far worse, maybe Charles Manson and his family found this place and stayed awhile. We do know that Manson and his family lived at Barker Ranch in Goler Washes, California. And we know that the road through Goler Washes eventually leads to Death Valley. The spooky Manson family most likely roamed freely in this area. The Manson family believed that Armageddon was about to destroy civilization, and they prepared for it.

Wikieup, Arizona, was our final stop just in time to help the good folks celebrate their annual rattlesnake round-up. Prize money was offered for the biggest rattlesnake and for the most snakes caught. Our restaurant offered rattlesnake steak—we declined.

It was good to be back among other people again and to see women. Our waitress was kind and gentle and it was good to hear her soft voice and smell her sweetness. It was also good to have our meals prepared for us. I thought about Doris. The world had not come to an end.

Written in 1982.

High Desert Gold

There is no greater freedom than the freedom to be who you are, where you are in this moment.

Without rain, the Death Valley desert was dry right up to where night reaches stars, up beyond a moon that filled the night. I smelled drifts of pollen and sage in the cup of my hand. During the day, the desert's hot breath was mineral cooking in the sun. Firewood was just outside a fire-ring of rocks.

Think a dinner-plate moon, golden, large enough to light the night and bright enough to read by. I looked about and saw silhouettes of thorny thickets and night animals moving in long shadows.

I envision a lone prospector and his trusted burro roaming the desert looking for rooster tails of quartz outcropping along the ridges of foothills and shoulders of mountains. I suspected his dream of finding gold and silver by experience, myth, intuition, or map, was more than a search for wealth and treasure; it was a search for his authentic self. And like a monk searching for holiness, and a medieval knight searching for the Holy Grail, this prospector searched for his authentic self in the deserts and mountains of the dry Southwest.

This wilderness that cupped Death Valley was both home and journey for this grizzled prospector. It led him to his private treasure. And when found he could not return to his yesteryears nor to where he was born.

Also, I suspect the reason he roamed the deserts and foothills was not so much for hidden treasure, but to fill his need for freedom and desert solitude.

Furthermore, I suspect this prospector's newfound gold gave him reason for a night in a saloon where friendly folks loosened his tongue with whisky and legally stole his claim with pen. This gave him reason to return to where he belonged.

He knew that gold would make him rich and also knew what gold could not buy. He knew following a promising vein too far through rock would lead him too deep into the mountain's heart, then enslave him to pick and shovel in carbide lamp light, in twilight dark.

Poverty set him free to wander untroubled by wealth, social connections, lawyers, and politics—worst of all. All he needed was a burro, sacks of beans, flour, and coffee, and a rifle for game and protection. He dreamed a pot of gold at the end of a rainbow, as legend taught was the gate of heaven. But he never came to the end of his rainbow. No one does. That was best of all.

Written in 2000.

Macho Tom

"Ignorant people think it's the noise which fighting cats make that is so aggravating, but it ain't so; it's the sickening grammar they use." Mark Twain

A wild and wooly kingdom of cats, skunks, snakes, toads, and other creatures live below my knees around our place. And flying creatures free and wild fly at will above my head. That leaves me with a middle kingdom I can say is civilized and domesticated.

Macho Tom and Fem Cat along with their feline society live in the lower regions.

Macho Tom—I don't know his given name nor if he has one—belongs to no one. He comes and goes as it suits his fancies, urges, and curiosities. His Westside kingdom is five square miles west of Interstate 17. I'm sure his kingdom is an exciting story of cats, kittens, and romances.

Furthermore, I suspect he keeps the cat population well stocked with his particular blend of genes whenever the opportunity arises. He's an alpha male cat by every definition. His fur is chinchilla gray and sheep-wool thick, offering a deep defense against the fangs and claws of rivals. One ear is chewed back half its length and his face is crisscrossed with battle scars of wins and losses.

His royal face is broad, Mongolian flat, with eyes that stare in no-nonsense confidence deep into the hearts of rivals and deep into the hearts of lovers.

Fem-Cat is queen cat in Westside cat society. When she's plump with kittens, Macho is not allowed around. But when she's inviting, Tom moves back for a while, and if any other tomcat shows up, a few laps around the barn with Tom in close pursuit, ending in the rafters, is enough to set things neatly back in place.

Night is when the cat kingdom is wild and furious. Cat sounds fill my sleeping hours with scuffling sounds, long piercing wails, and guttural jungle noises. Their socialization is well described; one evening a stray tomcat invaded Macho Tom's domain. At first Macho Tom flattened himself against the ground and slowly crawled toward the invader. After moaning wails—negotiation time—both cats raced toward each other and exploded into a fang and claw whirlwind, a hissing and spitting bouncing ball of tomcat-fury. They became a hairball of fighting cats, a two-cat-blur of gray and yellow fur, a two-foot tempest tomcat competition. They bounced about the front lawn, all the while screeching and filling the air with cat fur. As one dribbles a basketball, they dribbled themselves and then quickly disengaged, but not before they left behind a settling cloud of hair, an echo of what just happened.

The invading tomcat lost his romantic curiosity, courage, and a tolerable amount of hair, while Macho Tom retained his crown in his Westside kingdom. Neither cat seemed badly hurt, for these cats know when to hold and when to fold. The loser backed off and slipped away, and the winner was content to let the loser leave.

Remarkably, in spite of the fighting and arguments, there are still a lot of kittens in the Westside cat kingdom.

Last week a new sound was added to the usual noises of Westside cat society. A skunk moved in under our home and evicted Macho Tom and his family. The cats protested the intrusion, but the skunk won the argument. Peace came at last to the knee-high kingdom.

Under the back porch light I saw Macho Tom and his family patiently waiting the skunk's departure. I don't know when that happened. That's none of my business.

Macho Tom knows that when you battle a skunk, even if you win, you go away smelling like one. Macho Tom knows when to hold and when to fold.

Written in 2016.

Dog Days

"Brothers and sisters I bid you beware of giving your heart for a dog to tear." Rudyard Kipling

Summer dog days in the Verde Valley, days of sticky humidity called monsoon season with brief intermissions, usually begin in June and normally end in early September. They begin in morning, grow humid and hot to midday and afternoon. Winds grow, clouds boil, thunder booms, and silver lightening cracks sharp whips. Cool rain follows.

Late afternoons, the days become gentle and conceive rainbows born of light and mist. These sing in primary colors and misty tears of joy. The beauty and wonder of it makes mystics of sensitive souls.

These are days of slow-pitch softball, with fans supporting their teams. It's also a time when dogs find cool relief in shady places for afternoon siestas. Dogs know how to stay cool.

This is for people who know and love dogs. Dogs demonstrate devotion, dependency, and gratitude and have a way of getting into a person's heart.

Remarkably, dogs are content with just the crumbs that fall from tables. Consequently, they are so devoted and thankful for small fare they become faithful companions and pets for people of good will and ill will, too.

Sometime back, this dog story appeared in a prominent newspaper: A pet dog was lost near Tucson and the sad family searched and posted flyers, with no success. Finally the family lost hope and abandoned the search. They returned to their home in the state of Washington.

About a year later, so the story goes, foot sore, hungry, and lean, the dog arrived in the front yard of his home and after fixing a resentful stare in the direction of his dumbfounded family, resumed his doggie life.

Think about this: unless this dog's identity tag was a credit card for hitching rides, the dog had to travel through deserts, over mountains, negotiate highways, and fast traffic that lay between Tucson, Arizona and Washington.

No matter how the dog got home by foot, by car or someone's prank, it was a doggie miracle. For people who love dogs, anything a faithful dog will do to get home after being lost will bring a tear or two.

Written in 1998.

Dancing with Dogs

"But now ask the beasts, and let them teach you; and the birds of the heavens, and let them tell you." Job 12:7

The Romulus and Remus wolf myth was more than an ancient story for me; it was a story that joined me to animals, especially dogs. Furthermore, you could say that I was raised by these descendants of wolves, for dogs taught me work and rest, joy and sorrow, life and death, play and dance, and how to defend that which was important.

Therefore, I defer to no one in my knowledge and care of dogs. Once more, my bicycle tours and subsequent encounters with these animals should qualify me as a mediator between cyclists and dogs.

Dog trainers know that their students have wolves in their blood, and that they need a wolf pack's discipline, status, rewards, and meaningful work for them to be content.

Many once tended sheep and cattle, stood guard and pulled sleds; however, times have changed, though not for the betterment of dogs and people. Undisciplined and unemployed dogs tend to extend their territories, write their own job descriptions, and appoint themselves guardians of public places.

Dogs and cyclists go together, but not always in ways that are mutually beneficial. It's not that cyclists don't try to keep a safe distance between themselves and dogs; it's that some dogs don't cooperate. When that safe distance is breached, trouble begins.

There is something about a moving bicycle that transforms gentle Shep into an aggressive predator. Perhaps dogs are agitated by the hum of wheels or the hypnotic whisper of spokes, or the metallic whir of a chain over sprockets, or thin tires against pavements and gravel. Then again, it may be the illusion of a fleeing animal that kicks in the predatory instincts of dogs.

On our bicycle journey across America, my dog encounters were not all negatives. I laughed when little dogs on short legs tried to outrun me. And I was gratefully surprised when a couple of big hounds took one look at me and fled in the opposite direction. Most likely they knew pepper spray.

While cycling by a farm house in the Missouri Ozarks, three dogs charged. The lead dog vectored toward a spot up the road where he planned to engage me. Anticipating his tactics, I stopped while it raced to his intended confrontation. Of course, I wouldn't be there. The other two dogs stayed with me and watched. I'll always remember the surprised look on that dog's face when he discovered that he was up the road all by himself. I laughed when I saw his confidence melt into surprise and then collapse into embarrassment. Mustering as much dignity as he could, he trotted back and nipped my front tire, no harm done. In a dog's world, as it is with humans, saving face by having the last word is important, especially if you're the top dog. I laughed again, which didn't help. After sniffing around my leg to regain control, he gave me permission to move on.

I biked past gray-haired dogs—arthritic in joint—that merely lifted their heads and half-heartedly barked. Time and infirmities had rendered them as placid as five-bean salads. These old veterans of past bike wars were content to spend their golden years dreaming of exciting encounters. They reminded me of veterans of foreign wars, full of old war stories, basking in their twilight years. I'm confident that these old dogs had trained young dogs in the art of bicycle chasing and now they were content to leave the duty of protecting turf and territory to a younger generation.

Dancing with dogs was a necessary part of our sacred journey. They kept me wisely alert and wonderfully entertained with humorous moments, along with sudden jolts of terror and lingering plateaus of fear and anxiety. Once more, dogs contributed a special kind of animal wildness to my bike tour that I needed. I'm a wiser person for having danced with them.

The Story of Old Drum

Senator George Graham Vest in 1870 gave the finest dog tribute. On The Johnson County Missouri, Courthouse lawn, Old Drum stands guard on a granite pedestal with Vest's eulogy on a plaque. "Gentleman of the Jury, a man's dog stands by him in prosperity and in poverty, in health and in sickness. He will sleep on the cold ground, where the wintry winds blow and the snow drives fiercely, if only he may be near his master's side. He will kiss the hand that has no food to offer, he will lick the wounds and sores that he encounters in the roughness of the world. He guards the sleep of his pauper master as if he were a prince. When all other friends desert, he remains. When riches take wings and reputation falls to pieces, he is as constant in his love as the sun in his journey through the heavens. If fortune drives the master forth an outcast in the world, friendless and homeless, the faithful dog asks no higher privilege than that of accompanying him to guard against danger, to fight against his enemies. When the last scene of all comes, and death takes the master in his embrace and his body is laid away in the cold ground, no matter if all other friends pursue their way, there by his graveside will the noble dog be found, his head between his paws, his eyes sad but open in ever alert watchfulness, faithful and true even to death."

Written in 2000. This is an abridged version of "Dancing with Dogs," which is included fully in my book *Catching a Dream: A Sacred Bicycle Journey Across America.*

Canyon Flight

Anything we imagine, we can do—even fly

We made our plans to fly over the Grand Canyon. The 4:30 alarm signaled the beginning of this adventure. I am always eager to fly, and when invited to do so, my anticipation is that of a very happy small boy.

I picked up Charlie German at his home, drove to the Burgbacher Ranch, where we were joined by Nelson Harris. Standing next to the dirt runway, we waited for Ralph in his Piper Aztec to arrive from Phoenix. Soon we heard the faint hum of the plane and watched it slowly grow from a speck between mountains. It grew to a muffled roar as the plane circled, throttled back, sank to the narrow runway, its props kicking-up dust and dirt. It slowed to a soft stop. Ralph was ready to take us on a scenic ride over the Grand Canyon.

We boarded the plane, then waited while Ralph checked instruments. We watched the rpm needles rise to full power, then waited for the right moment to dash up into the sky.

Twin engines roared and the plane shivered like a race horse at the starting gate. After the props had pried us loose from gravity's Velcro, we scooted down the runway chased by a blizzard of dust and escaped into the sky.

We had traded earth's security for thin air and flight. It is a good trade. Up, up we climbed into the cool morning sky. Tipping a wing now and then, we viewed the winding Verde River, the patchwork of fields, puddles of ponds, and then Camp Verde and Cottonwood. Ralph punched flight coordinates into the autopilot and it set a north course for The Grand Canyon.

With gravity's invisible hand pressing down, never far from wings lifting up, never far from our aluminum bird—we flew.

Gravity waited for the sun to melt the Icarus wax of our wings, always critical and unforgiving, wanting us to fail, wanting to push us down where we belonged. Gravity doesn't want us to fly; she wants us on ground.

The autopilot guided us along an invisible line that began in our plane and ended in the Grand Canyon control tower. While we exchanged light-hearted comments and the Aztec's twin engines sang their sweet duet, our D.M.E. ticked off air miles to destination.

We flew above the Grand Canyon as an eagle flies; we soared in gentle sweeps and arcs in the thin air. Pink temple rocks jutted up from below like cathedral spires. Plateaus spread in jigsaws, while gray cloud shadows flowed in the inner canyon.

Way down deep in the bottom crease of the canyon, the Colorado River is a brown ribbon in the shadows and reflections. Hot thermals rose up in elevator currents, splashing against the Aztec's belly, bouncing us in sudden surprise. I asked Ralph if he would fly deeper into the canyon and he said, "I won't fly beneath the rim, for if an engine failed in this thin air, as heavy as we are, the Aztec wouldn't have enough lifting power to lift out of the Canyon. We would need to fly down the Colorado River to Lake Mead to land." Ralph knows his Aztec. He won't take chances.

We flew over the Supai Indian village on our return trip; then, after skirting the Bill William's fire tower, we toured the east face of Mingus Mountain. Heading home, we circled in from the south over Ralph's ranch—flaps down—slow descent, like a duck landing on water. In breezy whispers the

Aztec slipped under a hill, as an eagle comes to limb, spreading its wings, flaring its feathers, talons extended. We softly crunched down on the runway, scooted in short bursts of power, and slowed to a stop. Gravity sighed in relief.

A version of "Canyon Flight" was published as "Grand Canyon Flight" in the *Verde View,* August 1, 1978.

Up, Up And Away

The greatest dreams are always unrealistic. The song "Up, Up and Away" put words and music to the feeling of freedom and the joy of flying.

Ever since Daedalus in Greek myth made wings of beeswax and feathers for his son Icarus to escape imprisonment on Crete, men have envisioned escaping earth by flying weightlessly in the sky.

Unfortunately, as the story unfolds, Icarus flew too high and the sun melted the wax that held feathers to his wings and he fell to the sea and drowned. Flying and falling still happens. A Greek myth doesn't have to be true to be true.

Jerry Byler dreamed of flying, too, but unlike most of us he put his dreams into practice and now flies. He's not sitting in the pilot's seat of a 747, he's sitting in an ultralight motorized glider alone in the sky.

If you happen to look up someday and wonder where that strange buzzing sound is coming from and see what appears to be a cross between a kite and a Piper J-3-Cub, it's probably Jerry in his motorized hang glider. With a fresh wind in his sails, hanging up there under the air frame, suspended by two straps, a nylon seat, Jerry is able to maneuver his lightweight craft through a sea of air. For some time now, Jerry has been seen soaring with the hawks over the canyons of Oak Creek and riding the thermals that rise up out of the Verde Valley.

At times I've thought of being up there along with Jerry in my own flying machine. But the cost of a motorized hang glider runs over $2,000, too much money at the moment. That financial weight is more than enough to keep me on the ground.

While serving in the Air Force in the late 1940s, I flew as a passenger in C-47 cargo planes lumbering from country to country over the Pacific, and in commercial and private planes afterward, but I have yet to know the freedom of solo flights in a tubular steel airframe covered with nylon pushed by a very small motorcycle engine. I suppose this dream will end up in the same dream bin as my dreams of parachuting, sailing a boat to Hawaii, and biking across the country.

I did bike across the county in 1985. One out of four isn't bad.

It's good to see Jerry in the sky doing his dream. I can't come up; he can't come down.

Last Tuesday I visited Jerry's flying machine and carefully examined it part by part, testing its tendon wires and tough nylon wing material with my fingers. My thoughts turned to the Greek myth of Icarus and his feathered wings. But Jerry Byler's glider is more than wax and feathers. His flying machine is well designed and has been tested for many years.

His sister told me this story: A summer thunderstorm in the Verde Valley brewed a rising thermal and caught Jerry. Up, up and away he flew until Squaw Peak lay beneath him. By the way, Squaw Peak is the official name of a mountain in the center of Arizona that overlooks the Verde Valley; however, the PC police have corrected it. Now it's just Peak in polite society—dull, and neutral.

Unable to nose his tiny craft down against the rising thermal, in desperation he shut off its engine, but it made no difference. He continued to rise out of control. It is dangerously cold at that altitude. To make matters worse, his tiny glider accelerated to fifty miles per hour.

Finally, he flew outside the thermal and spiraled back to earth. Landing, he rolled out of the glider and lay still, cold, unable to stand.

Again, one morning in Oak Creek Village where he lives, Jerry took off, misjudged his altitude and flew into electrical lines which shut down the power grid. The good people of Oak Creek Village were not happy with Jerry and his glider that morning when they couldn't watch television nor fix breakfast. That's the price Jerry pays for his flying adventure.

How does Jerry's family feel about his flying? I met with them and we talked about Jerry and his flying glider, and I came away with a colorful collection of feelings, concerns, and opinions. They all agreed that Jerry is doing what he wants to do and they support him. Jerry needs to be in the air and they want him on the ground. They can't go up and he can't come down. That's the price Jerry and his family pay for his flying. Jerry is an eagle flying and his family won't put him in their cage.

Go with God, Jerry Skywalker, and may the Force be with you.

Written in 2000.

The Scout Master

Somewhere in the night a khaki-shirted man stands watch over a troop of scouting boys. Campfires have burned to embers. A full moon is the nightlight. Shadows slowly measure the earth's rotation and the moon's orbit, while the Milky Way, salted with stars, arches and swings across the heavens. Constellations become silent tick-tocks of the universe's celestial clock.

Under the green canopy of summer trees or huddled in the frosted tents of a winter camp, the age-old patterns of scouting are at the work of turning boys into men. The first night out, a troop seldom sleeps before midnight.

Free of parental oversight, the boys whisper boy-talk and explore the beginning edge of their manhood. They trade secrets and discoveries far into the night. They whisper and laugh until they tire of secrets and jokes.

These boys are beginning to investigate morality, even spirituality. They may have fresh response to reality, even thoughtful silences and absorption. But all these qualities are often dimmed by group-think, by fears, anxieties, and the moment's need to make sense of that which comes from all directions.

An off-key, off-beat coyote chorus yip-yaps in the near distance, accompanied by the piercing scream of its star soloist. It sounds as if the noises are coming from just behind the trees. It cuts the night like a serrated knife sawing glass, startling rabbits and boys. The hunting coyote pack, a hooting owl, the shrill "bree-bree" of tree frogs, and chirping and buzzing insects blend with nameless fears. A tenderfoot

Scout pulls back the entrance flap of his tent and sees the Scoutmaster by the fire. All's well. He goes back to sleep.

The khaki-shirted man moves about the camp, checking on his boys, each cocooned in a sleeping bag, each growing into a man. Some sleeping bags hold skinny-limbed and bony-chested kids, growing too fast for the luxury of fat and muscle. Others are still butterball-smooth, for their pituitaries had not yet signaled their pubescent changes. Older boys, beginning to grow upper-lip fuzz too fine for a razor's edge, talk about girls.

Scouting teaches a boy discipline, responsibility, hard work, beauty and ugliness, and life and death in the wild. Boys learn to live in the real world of dirt and wind, rain and snow, heat and cold. They learn that their bodies were fashioned in crucibles of seasons, in raw elements, and the wild kingdom that rewards intelligence and won't suffer fools gladly. It's real life beyond TV, computers, cell phones, and the internet.

They soon will learn what they need to know to survive and succeed in human society, but in the wild what is needed to survive is hard to find and hard to use. The Almighty's servant, Mother Nature, does not spoil her children. God forgives, but Nature doesn't.

Scouts learn how to pitch a tent in wind, snow and rain. They learn how to carry a five-day supply of food and needful miscellany on their backs. They learn the taste of salty sweat in June on a long hot hike into the Grand Canyon, where mules have the right of way, and the way out of the Canyon up a steep dirt trail step by step a few days later.

Furthermore, they discover to their surprise that cuts and bruises, even blisters, sweat and exhaustion are not preludes to dying, but rather character- and stamina-building experiences.

But first this khaki-shirted man, this master of boys, must first be mastered before he has the right to help boys discover their manhood. He may have been drafted by a desperate troop committee, or he may have been concerned with the needs of someone's son, or his own. Whatever the beginning, the making of a Scoutmaster depends on his decency and dedication to Scouting and respect for boys and their aspirations. If he can understand and endure, better yet join, the restless energies of prankish boys without losing his patience and temper, he can wear his uniform proudly. If he is able to juggle the time demands on his private life, the calendar of scout meetings and outings, and his job or profession, he can lead his boys. If he can remain committed during the dull and discouraging times when neither he nor his boys can be prodded into effort, during the hectic scramble for adult help, trip transportation, money, and the lead-heavy hike up mountain trails, then he will be called a leader of boys.

He pulls off his blister-making boots and sighs. "I've just got to find a younger man to take my place." But when he never quite gets around to finding another man, he has passed his severest test, his master's degree in Scouting.

Scouting is not all trial and testing, it's fun and food, and learning, too. When a Tenderfoot eagerly plans in detail his first overnight camping trip and when that First Class Scout suddenly comes alive to the challenge of the merit badge and skill awards and begins his climb to the lofty rank of Eagle Scout; and when his boys stand in troop formation, patrol beside patrol, in pride and dignity, beyond their years, then he knows he can't quit, not this year anyway.

Our Scoutmaster is a man living his boyhood once again and finding the meaning of his past. He is Robinson Crusoe and Hiawatha, mother and father, drill sergeant and counselor to his boys. He must have the patience of Job, the humor of Red Skelton, and the endurance of a long distance runner. He must forgive like a saint, and exercise the wisdom of King Solomon. He must be able to sleep on rocks, sample an eleven-year-old boy's first meal cooked over a campfire, survive a five-day hike with fifteen boys, and return them all safe and sound to their parents without hatching a covey of ulcers. He must be willing to schedule his scouting meetings and activities around his work without jeopardizing his income, and put on hold his free time, his home life, and his wife and a soft bed for the priorities of Scouting. And, if he is fortunate, he will have a wife who will send him off with a smile and welcome him home with a hug, a kiss, and a twinkle in her eye.

The Scoutmaster's reward for his calling is the satisfaction of helping parents guide their sons through the twists, turns, and confusions of growing into good and responsible manhood.

When the time comes for him to turn over his troop to a younger man, he must know how to step away and continue to guide his boys by example and inspiration. He must be content to be a good and positive memory when boys become men. If time robs him of his memory, he must know that his boys will never forget him.

Then, when our Scoutmaster stands in attention before the inevitable inventory of his life, when he is full of years and wisdom, when he has clear hindsight, and when he is reminded day and night of his humanity, he then must be confident that the good that he did and the success that came from it far outweighs his mistakes and regrets.

Furthermore, he must be convinced that his work with boys made more sense than uninvolved complaining, and that what happened in his troop made a big difference for good in the lives of his boys, his community, and his country.

Finally, he must know that "All things work together for good to them who love God, to those who are called according to His purposes." Romans 8:28.

When his golden years turn platinum, and his memories blur and fade, the Scoutmaster still remembers and lives his Scout Oath and Creed, for it is marbled deep within his soul and in his bone: "On my honor I will do my best, To do my duty to God and my county, and to obey the Law; To help other people at all times; To keep myself physically strong, mentally awake and morally straight."

I know this is true. I have been a Scoutmaster in the best years of my life.

A version of "The Scout Master" was published in the *Verde View,* February 13, 1979.

Visitors

There's urgency in the forest now and the deer know it; they nervously browse the oaks for acorns and leaves. Soon frost will kill weeds and grass, and oaks will sing a chorus of color against silent evergreens.

Deer know the coming winter will barren trees and bury acorns and autumn leaves beneath snow and ice. Cold nights will chill oak wood and send sap into the security of their roots. Before snow is deep under a crust of ice, the deer will move down among the cedars to winter in deep canyons. But for now, they move slowly—gray shadows in oak groves—searching.

It had rained in the forest the first part of last week, thus fire-proofing the forest floor, as if a wet quilt had been thrown down, smothering what sparks of life remained. Now it is safe to build cooking and warming fires.

Scout Troop 11 took to the woods last Friday after school for a night and day in the forest. We set up tents near an oak grove, then built a stone circle for a cooking fire. We ate dinner and then built a warming fire that burned a warm hole in the cold evening. It is a dancing fire that kindles a boy's thoughts and imagination—better than TV.

Far into the night the boys talked and laughed, as boys do when free to share what each had learned, what each must know before he becomes a man. Every man begins as a boy. When lethargy silenced the boys, they crawled into their tents and cocooned themselves into sleeping bags. The campfire died, the circle of rocks grew cold, and I stood guard through the night half-awake until first light.

We are alien visitors, guests among ponderosa pines and acorn oaks, visiting this world more hostile than the boys could know. We brought food and shelter and fire from our other world. We came from just twenty miles away and arrived as time-travelers from a distant future, not in miles but in centuries of time. We would return home from this world of oak and deer before the next day turned old. We are guests, not citizens of this distant past.

For deer and oaks this was home. They knew winter was coming and knew the need to store fat beneath their skins, just as oaks know to store sap deep in in their roots.

The morning sun spread patches of light among the oaks and under our ponderosa ceiling. These patches grew into shafts and spread as liquid heat, seeping into tents and sleeping bags, rousing boys, and warming stiffened joints.

We dressed, then shivered through a pancake breakfast, bacon and eggs, and for some, coffee too.

Now the boys began to know the urgency of late fall as the deer know. Yet, still, they also know that they are from another place and time and would soon go home.

The boys played in the forest with ax, bow, and a sheath of arrows. They played as visitors play when they visit the exciting unknown. They shot target arrows into stumps and against armored trees and up into the open sky. They talked of hunting deer and bear. Boys live in their imagination. What they believe becomes true.

We hiked several miles into the woods and hunted in groves of oaks, measuring distances by arrow flight.

We thought of Indian boys of long ago, who hunted deer from these same groves, ancestors of the deer we now see. Our bows were not hunting bows and our arrows were just toys and the deer knew this and silently slid out of sight to eat acorns from another grove.

We came upon a hunting camp near a forest road, and by hunter's code, we kept fifty yards away, the courtesy we give to peaceful bears. It's cluttered with hunting stuff: boxes of food, folding chairs, and bedding made into rolls, all things of another world, our world too.

They were day-by-day hunters and if this camp remained forgotten, it would soon be covered with coming snow and buried under years of seasons, growth, and decay. That's the way it is in this other world of oaks and deer. Nature will scab and heal this forest land.

In the distance a rifle shot poked a sharp hole in the silence. It's a sound unlike an arrow leaving a bow. These hunters were visitors in this forest of long ago. Out of time, out of tune, out of place. They and we could not stay, perhaps for them a week.

The boys had played as Apache boys once played among these trees. Soon, the boys were tired from too much night and too little sleep. Time and place ruled our day. Our food was low and we could not stay. We drove the fire back into the earth and walked away.

We left the deer to play their ancient game of hide and seek, as their ancestors did among the oaks.

We, too, had played the ancient game while searching for meaning of our lives.

The deer sank deeper into their woods and we sank deeper into our future life.

A version of "Visitors" was published as "The Aliens" in the *Verde View*, November 21, 1979.

January Rain

Dark clouds heavy with Pacific moisture lifted from that birthplace of storms. They come heavy with moisture in eastbound winds, then climb the Sierras and dump water in California, Arizona, and New Mexico. Then they race across Oklahoma and Kansas. Lighter, faster, and leaner, they race to the eastern seaboard and drop what's last left in rain or snow. Sometimes they are pushed south by Arctic storms.

These January storms march in line across Arizona, like elephants crossing the African veldt. They muddy the land and fill their footprints with standing water, filling cattle tanks, soaking sandy washes, and turning the forest floor into spongy, leafy-beds. All living things rejoice.

The black clouds of January veil the winter sun, hiding light under thick winter hide. Addicted to sun, we hope for sun each day, only to find a lowering gloom; although we do need rain and snow.

Winter rains, snow, and ice in the mountains will fill our aquifers and turn streams into rivers. White Mountain trout streams will rush against their rocks and banks.

Winter rains came to the Verde Valley last week. They came to restore moisture in the deep roots of catclaw and mesquite. Spring bees will carry catkins of nectar to their hives and make honey. Pacific water becomes honey.

To the north, fifty miles to Flagstaff, a mammoth winter storm covered the city and forest with a blanket of snow, folding drifts into fences. The Snow Bowl will fill with skiers who will ride the lift to the top and ski down, thanks to Pacific water.

Our goats lay in dry straw in their barn, while bees cluster around their honey, brood, and queen. Our wood stove keeps the cold beyond windows.

We live in the Verde Valley, elevations beneath Flagstaff. I would like to see these winter storms turn rain into snow. I would like to awaken tomorrow morning in a Michigan winter where I was born.

A version of "January Rain" was published in
Verde View, on January, 17, 1980.

El Toro Storms

Unlike January storms, El Toro storms of summer are Bravo fighting bulls. They trot up from the Gulf of Mexico into the arena of southwest Arizona. And unlike slow moving elephant storms of winter that stay for days, these bulls snort, charge and blow their strength away in a single day.

El Toro storms charge in gusts of wind and dust and strut back and forth in the Verde Valley arena. In the humid heat of monsoon they lay corn fields on their sides, then shake fruit from trees, sometimes de-limb cottonwood and sycamore trees.

They charge and snort and gore trees with lightning horns, setting them afire. Their tossing muscles fly rainbowed banderoles of animal power.

At last a red sunset cape deceives and a final lightning sword pierces their hearts. They bleed in sunset blood.

They never die. El Toro Bravo will be back to fight another day.

Written in 2000.

Monarch Ponderosa

One summer evening, long ago, while driving up the Coronado Trail in Arizona, Doris and I found ourselves in a violent summer storm. This storm climbed mountain slopes on lightning legs and randomly struck snags and living trees.

Suddenly, near our road, a ponderosa pine exploded in a flash of lightning. In a micro-second this monarch tree lost its crown and life below. This lightning sword had cut a deep gash down its side from crown to root.

One moment the tree was in full glory, head and shoulders above all; the next moment it was lightning struck in wooden shock.

The assassin's sword in thunder's sheath had waited eighty years for this moment to happen. I felt that sword in my heart.

It was raining hard. The monarch's crown of emerald jewels lay scattered on the ground. The stunned tree smoldered in smoke, in tears of rain.

Insects and diseases will have their way. Woodpeckers will bore nesting holes. Hawks and eagles will watch for prey from its crownless top, while sun and winds will bleach and dry its wooden bones.

In a final lightning strike its *coup de grâce* will explode again in blazing chunks, as one scatters embers from a fireplace. We smelled the incense of last rites. Later, Nature will do her mortician's work in a recycling liturgy, and its descendants will grow in ashes.

Softly, the wind will chant ashes to ashes, dust to dust,"The Lord gives, The Lord takes away, blessed be the name of the Lord." Job 1:21.

Written in 2000.

The Rainbow

A rainbow touched the Valley last week. This rainbow was born of light and water. I watched it slowly drift through a mesquite field, and when its colors drifted through a single tree, it blazed with cold fire. Then the rainbow drifted beyond a ridge and became only light.

It's easy to know why ancients believed a rainbow was a message of hope from God. Thunder, lightning, and flood had retreated, leaving a promise of good things to come.

It's also easy in our scientific enlightened age to reduce a rainbow to prismatic laws. In this explanation, how easy to pause and say "Oh look, there's a rainbow," then move on without stopping to listen to its message in the heart.

I agree with science's soft war between rationality and ignorance, between reason and superstitions, and between truth and fake science.

This I believe: to be truly human in our search for truth and the meaning of life, we must ask questions and always search for more than we know. Do rainbows still drift through human hearts with the promise that when a storm is over good times will come? Mystics say yes. I say yes, too.

The mystical meanings of rainbows rightfully belong to poets, children, artists, and pious folks who still see wonder in ordinary things. For them, divine appearances, holy wonders, and epiphanies do come. This is the rainbow in the heart. I am at home in this group.

An ordinary rainbow touched the earth last week and ordinary trees flamed in celestial glory. Ordinary people stopped to watch God hiding in plain sight.

A version of "The Rainbow" was published as "Rainbow" in *The Journal* in 1984.

Art

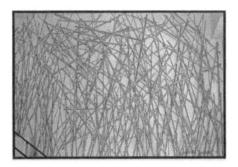

"Art is concerned not with botany but with flowers, not with root causes but with ultimate values, not with sex but with love, not with human nature but with human beings."
Gerald Bullett

Art is a jealous mistress. It's true. If I don't notice her, she nags me to distraction. And if I don't give her full attention, she turns her back and abandons me to just plain facts; then she flirts in walled art to get my attention.

I've visited the Crystal Bridge Museum of American Art in Bentonville, Arkansas several times. Here I can view mega dollars of famous art treasure for free. I could set up a tent and live there.

Though money buys expensive art, it comes with the fear of theft, flood, and fire. Many owners secure their art in humidity and temperature controlled museums with security guards, then hang art prints at home. Some guests and thieves don't know the difference; those who do, keep respectfully quiet.

I store my art in archival 300-year Gold CD-R discs. A few pieces hang on walls, most in memory. I don't worry about theft. No one wants to buy nor steal my art.

No price tag makes art good. Art is a lady; she can't be bought. At her best she's the fluid freedom of visual speech. She may bless good copy work, random smearing and splashing paint. Advertising art may give her a second look. Modern art may move her mind and heart. She's in camera realism and illusion on Photoshop's paper.

She hides in stone, wood, iron or anything else in the artist's insight. She's hammer and chisel birthing a statue from marble and wood. She may be the soul of sculptures, carvings, and scrap iron monuments, or she may reject the most inventive work of professionals, leaving it soulless.

Art is frozen cold in deep winter—yet beckons in snow, ice-frosted evergreens groves of bare-limbed sycamores asleep in their deep roots.

She plays in forest, deer, birds, and the artist's joy of seeing. Then, in sudden inspiration, she comes from eyes to heart and pours her life into brush, painting knife, and paint.

When her mood changes from love to fickle indifference, she can't be found and her lover searches in vain, calling in the night.

She may hide for days when I need her most. In that dark night when her moon is covered, when my last work of art was stillborn, when fear whispers, "I've lost her forever," she comes in soft pastels of hope.

To list a couple of her successful lovers: Monet's "The Magpie," "Waterloo Bridge Misty Morning," and "Dreamy Water Lilies."

Manet's "Woman Pouring Water," and his "In The Conservatory."

Van Gogh's "Edge of a Wheat Field with Poppies" and "Wheat Field with a Lark," "The Good Samaritan," and "Blossoming Almond Tree."

She's history alive in "Sioux Wigwams in a Cottonwood Grove." She's history in Russell's and Remington's landscapes, cowboys and Indians, forts and cavalry.

Not to forget modernism's mirrored glass in which we see ourselves. There's more than money can buy, but free to those who visit museums and view ordinary prints.

Art is a water nymph dancing and laughing in fluid grace down moss-covered travertine rocks.

Art is a writer's inspiration, a sculptor's stone, an architect's design.

Art is seeing the unusual in the usual, beauty in the homely, truth in honesty. Even ugliness deserves a second look. Again and again Art reminds us that beauty is in the eye of the beholder.

Art is common cobblestones, steel and glass skyscrapers bordered by traffic lights, streetlights, and parking meters. She's a cruising patrol car, an ambulance, a fire engine, and ghetto children sitting on apartment steps. She's a single face in a crowded rush hour.

Art cries in a skid row derelict and a homeless bag lady with all her possessions in a shopping cart aimlessly wandering dirty back streets among trashcans. She's a living story of journeys far from home. She's a little girl and boy lost in misbegotten dreams.

Art is a new baby in the arms of a young mother. She peeks coyly under a little girl's bonnet. Anywhere innocent truth is found, art is there. She's in youth and in the wise faces of grandmothers and grandfathers.

Art sees wonder in new snow, old shoes, old trumpets, and the new-start promise of a just born baby.

Art can be a poet's choice of words that sing and teach between lines, and in novels that give hope and strength in life's long journeys.

Art always finds a way.

Written in 2015.

The Dark of December

In this dark December morning, before the stir of busy people, my thoughts turn to family, friends, and to you.

From my warm office window, I see a silver sheen of frost on the lawn, while our trees sleep in the single night-light of a soft street lamp. A cold sun struggles to be dawn.

This is the season of remembrance and for touching what is most important.

My life began a movie. Each day is a frame now running in the world's theater. I note my transformations over time. It will end in my departure. I am not the person I was.

I remember my family and friends, along with the bittersweet frost of loss and loneliness. I think of my childhood and my youth, my Doris and our children, and scatterings of loves I once held close to my heart and still do.

We are taught that all must pass away into yesterday's memories and that all must become new today. There must be a tomorrow. It is true. God loves us too much for anything to stay and anyone to remain. Unlike the scattering of spent leaves in a cold fall wind lost in drifts of snow, then forgotten, my scattering and losses are remembered. It must be so, the wise say. I wonder.

Friends and families do pass away and all things become new. This I know that their replacement never comes. And this I also know, this is the season of cheer and good will. Nevertheless, beneath words of comfort and cheer, in the mists of tears, nostalgia is real in winter's night.

Maybe it's a longing for the sun and the warmth of a longer day, maybe missing a wife or husband too soon gone away. Perhaps a childhood remembered, or a grandmother in tears watching from her window for someone gone long ago.

This I know, though we live East of Eden, we still live, move, and have our being in God, who loves us as we are and who we will become.

In the dark of this December morning, this cold Christmas Day, my thoughts of loved ones run deep, clear, and bright as rainbowed Christmas lights, all strung against the shadowed greens and dark of my Christmas tree. This I know, this I believe, Faith, Hope, and Love are marbled in my bones in this winter of my years.

I will rejoice this day in what God has made.

Written in 2016.

Knoll Lake

I can go anywhere in the world from Camp Verde, Arizona, which makes my home the center of everywhere.

Charles Finley and Ralph Bloomquist, like-minded friends, invited me to join them for a couple of days at Knoll Lake. It is an easy offer to accept, not only for fishing but also for mental renewal. A couple of days at this mountain lake will be good for what ails me and needs fixing. I never quite know what ails me; however, I'm reasonably sure that a couple of days in the wilderness will find it and fix it.

At Knoll Lake campground, our Golden Eagle Pass plus two dollars each secured a Knoll Lake campsite. We pushed our campsite number and money in a drop-box and settled in. That first day someone with a badge, a clipboard, and a Big Brother smile walked by.

Faithfully, our campground host checked our campsite each day to make sure we had registered and had deposited our litter and money in the right places.

We saw several signs screaming in big red letters: "Extreme Fire Danger," "No Camp Fires in Undesignated Areas" and "No Fireworks." I broke dry pine needles between my fingers and found it true. I also knew our campground host and Forest Ranger would be watchful and edgy. Understandably, during fire season these good folks who watch over our wilderness real estate are compelled by experience to view all hikers and campers as walking matchsticks waiting to strike and burn the forest to ashes. Also, campers were forbidden to make excessive noise between ten p.m. and six a.m. Another great idea: Wild parties and wailing pop music makes sleep impossible. We were warned to keep dogs on leashes—not a bad idea. The irony of being bitten by a pet while visiting the home of wolves, bears, and rattlesnakes is enough to make a saint laugh to tears.

Most people who use the forest are law-abiding, but a pyromaniac will occasionally drift through. Many good people are just as dangerous and a few even believe that the "Extreme Fire Danger" signs are a threat to their Constitutional rights and don't think beyond cigarettes, campfires, burgers on a grill, and marshmallows on a stick.

Written in 1978.

Chevelon Canyon

Knoll Lake is temptingly close to Chevelon Canyon; therefore, I excused myself from my friends and slipped away for a visit to this canyon and trout stream. What Walden Pond was to Thoreau, Chevelon is to me.

Chevelon Canyon had a few fire warning signs tacked to trees, but no watchers with clipboards, money envelopes, drop-boxes, and no video surveillance—not yet. For good reason, a hike down into the canyon is too much work for most people and not worth the trouble for terrorists, having not yet found religious, political, and business targets worth blowing up. There is only wonder and beauty calming the heart.

My introduction to Chevelon Canyon goes back to the early 1960s when a friend in Winslow whispered about this secret Chevelon Canyon and trout stream. He said that an untamed stream runs through the canyon, which supports a lush habitat for beaver, black bear, rattlesnake, deer, and elk, complemented by a long list of life forms happily eating each other for lunch. Wild trout live there. Rainbow and German Brown trout thrive in this wild stream joyfully eating insects and each other.

Then my friend confided that the canyon had become too wild and dangerous for him. He became concerned about slick rocks and rattlesnakes, and he had begun to complain to his wife about the steep climb out and his shortness of breath. His wife had always worried about him going into the canyon alone. She worried that a snake bite or a broken leg deep in this remote canyon would quickly turn from a serious injury to a life-threatening emergency before help arrived. They echoed each other's fears. She insisted he stop going. He decided to stop going. As all well-married men know, a happy wife is a happy husband. But before he hung up his boots and fly rod, he felt the need to pass his secret canyon on to a younger man. That is me.

Unlike human habitat, Chevelon Canyon left alone remains in the care of Nature, changing year after year for the good of all.

Unfortunately, the steep climb, rattlesnakes, and slippery rocks are but modest barriers to human interference. Recently a new dam blocks Chevelon Creek downstream, forming Chevelon Canyon Lake and a primitive road makes the lake accessible to the public. That's bad news for Nature and purists like me. Maybe the lake is a plus— time will tell. But for now, the dam is an insult to the natural order of things. Water wants to be free; therefore, Nature will try to remove the dam and set it free. It will someday, unless maintained. The Earth is patient and always wins.

On the surface, predator and prey, keep predation and reproduction in competitive balance. The center holds. The Divine Conductor keeps the flow of life tuned and in harmony. Sometimes thunder drums and cymbals clash in lightning, a clear and present danger of death and flooding. Other times violins and flutes sing in birds.

For these experiences, a visitor can return year after year, decade after decade and experience raw wilderness with its seasonal adjustments of mineral, flora, and fauna.

Civilization and human habitats change slowly, sometimes terrifyingly suddenly and sometimes finally. Human nature guarantees this, unless the Divine Conductor stops the orchestra and disciplines its most destructive predator. Each time I go down into Chevelon Canyon, it's like going home again. This is where God hides in plain sight.

I visit my wild friends and their descendants—mostly the same. We don't talk much, nor need to. They have their ways, I have mine; they speak in sounds and movements. I have my language, too. We respect each other and that's enough for both of us.

Unfortunately, there are changes from those early years when I first heard of this enchanting place. There's more foot traffic and fewer trout. Each time I go down, I see deeper footpaths along the bank and more Velveeta Cheese boxes and salmon eggs in the water, a sure sign of meat fishermen. I walk into tangles of monofilament fish lines woven like spiders webs in the willows. And each time I fished, I caught fewer bold fish. The last time I went down, I returned without fish.

I'm confident that the Silent Accountant is still keeping honest records and that the book of life will eventually balance.

Though I had Chevelon's Eden sans the serpent, I did have a few parishioners critique my time away from pastoral duties. "Fishing too much," they murmured. Not true. Nevertheless, it is enough for a vague Christian guilt—my personal serpent hissing. After a 24/7 week of ministry among needy people, my day in the canyon is good medicine.

Faithfully, the canyon and stream healed my soul and my serpent slithered away.

I will always carry memories of those early times when insect hatches in the evening made trout bold and brought them boiling to the surface after a muddler minnow or a peacock lady tied on a #14 hook. I tied my own flies back then. In last-light I often caught slab-sided trout just minutes away from darkness. So faint the light I dared not lose a fly to a bold trout for fear I could not see well enough to tie another on a hair-thin tippet.

The last time I visited Chevelon Canyon, the beaver were still there. They still swam and splashed in the pools. I saw a black bear on my way out. He cut across the trail just ahead of me. And I heard the calls of wild turkeys coming to roost in ponderosa pines.

Old Chevelon is locked in memory. I will never lose it. My body was young then, my senses were sharp, and my thoughts ran clear and clean. That memory is still new, pristine and very good.

Finally, Chevelon Canyon has not lost its enchantment. It's Eden in my heart.

Written in 2016.

Five Pounds

My thoughts drift into summer greens and autumn's colorful oaks along lakes and stream banks.

Autumn fish grow bold in September. They know feeding time is short for storing winter fat. They boldly hunt and dimple their feeding pools and streams, hungrily gorging on late season moths and grasshoppers. Big bugs and big fish go together. It's time for me to tie deer hair muddler minnows and grasshopper imitations.

I plan to take a September fishing trip to Chevelon Canyon Creek for a date with autumn trout before freezing nights kill bugs and snow and ice send the big trout into winter's hiding.

Five Pounds is a fantasy trout that swims in my imagination. That's the one that lurks under stream banks and near swift-water rocks. That's the one that fights hard, won't give up, and gets away.

I'm going after my Five Pounds trout this month. And if I don't catch him, the fresh air, and the sights and smells of autumn will be worth the trip.

Some time ago, I composed a poem in tribute to my fantasy trout, the one who taught the fly and hook course at the pool's elementary.

Five Pounds Poem

Five Pounds, rainbowed trout,
A trout with a PhD,
Lives in myth, in my poetry,
In forest stream and pond.

He taught the fly-hook course,
At the pool's elementary,
And each spring in forest realm,
He gathered class around,
And studied fishermen,
From towns around.

A teacher whipped a dry fly close,
Peacock Lady finely wound,
He wrapped himself in it,
Snagged it where willows grow.

Fishermen stopped to look.
From towns around.

After a wary swim around,
He gulped a floating worm,
Again in hook scared snout,
A hook sunk deep and firm.

Cutting pool, rainbow shark,
Fighting hook worm had brought,
Under roots, around big rocks,
Rainbow lightning, watery sparks.

Fishermen stopped to look,
From towns around.

Panting heaving, ebbing strength,
Looping the line, tying a knot,
One last leap, one last swat,
Five Pounds won his fight.

Fishermen stopped to look,
From towns around.

Panting heaving, snout hook-sore,
From his watery home,
Five Pounds vowed, never again,
Never ignore,

A barefoot boy,
With cane-joined pole.

Written in 2016.

Potato Lake

Potato Lake is at the end of rough dirt road among towering ponderosa on the Mogollon Rim in Arizona. Centuries ago, so I'm told, a meteorite blasted the crater that now holds Potato Lake.

Tuffy Peach, our local historian, told me that early settlers grew potatoes near the lake, hence the origin of the name. These Mogollon spuds cooked up into tasty dinners. Tuffy also said that just down from Potato Lake, a Dutchman by the name of Van Falsent had a place called Poverty Flats where he worked hard keeping his family fed by hunting and growing potatoes and whatever else he could coax to grow above and below ground on his homestead.

Van Falsent is gone, potatoes are no longer grown here, and Poverty Flats has since surrendered to the forest, but Potato Lake remains.

Tuffy told me that Potato Lake was formed by a meteorite the size of a man's head. Who knows its origin, or what celestial beginnings destined it to blaze through our atmosphere and explode on earth. This we do know: tugged and pulled by stars, planets, and moons, the meteor followed the gravitational contours of space until earth pulled it into a collision course. It came destined to plunge down upon the trees and rocks of the Mogollon Rim. It arrived on time. A meteorite that size would have been nickel and iron, heavy as the darkness between the stars. This meteorite from deep space would come with a mass magnified by 40,000 miles per hour. To back up his claim, Tuffy quoted geological evidence that meteorite craters have been found all over the Mogollon Rim country, and Potato Lake is one of them.

Looking into the star-filled night, I imagine the meteorite curving in from space and striking the Earth's atmospheric shield in a shower of fire. Its massive energy blasts a crater, a half mile across, who knows how deep. Felling trees, setting instant fires, it pounds earth and rock into molten pudding; continuing on it shatters sandstone and limestone bedrock. Finally it scatters pebbles of nickel and iron. Its celestial journey ends at the bottom of what is now Potato Lake. What stories it could tell.

This meteorite scenario is most likely the beginning of Potato Lake; although less romantic souls say the lake's crater is merely a sinkhole caused by the collapse of underlying sandstone structure. When given a choice between a celestial visitor and a sink hole, I prefer the meteor. It doesn't need to be true to be true.

Last week, along with a couple of Scouts, I drove to Potato Lake for a day and night of camping. Wintertime at Potato Lake is a scene that deserves a photo insert in a January calendar. White aspens stand tall and stately along the south shore and cast long shadows over the frozen lake. Beyond a rim of wild grasses, ponderosa pines give the sloping banks a solemn green background.

We camped on the north side of the lake where deep snow hides in cold shadows.

Under the spell of a full moon, this meteorite crater is a chalice holding a mystery in snow and ice, a holy communion celebrating the union of heaven and earth.

Is it not reasonable to believe that something from heaven lies broken just beneath our feet?

Written in 2016.

Living Water

Our son, John, called the other day from Redding, California and we talked about their swimming pool. Doris and I have seen it. Nice pool.

John said the pool's water has never been changed, at least to his knowledge—for good reason. To empty a pool at the wrong time in Redding, California, subjects it to damage. Ground water pressure will lift an empty pool a foot or two, cracking the concrete. However, at certain times of the year when ground water level is low, a pool can be safely emptied. Most people never drain their pools, except for repairs, consigning their pools to a lifetime of chemicals and filters, adding water at the rate of evaporation.

I thought about this swimming pool for some time and this thought crystallized: Water is wild in a poetic way. And as wild things like water, grasslands, rivers, forests, deserts, and animals are most alive and enjoyable when they are left to their wildness. Once we control them, they become problems. In spite of our good intentions, what we control will weaken, change and die unless we place them on artificial support.

Pools are refreshing and healthful, bringing into our backyards water that once was wild. Though serene and beautiful in evening light, though exciting when in use, there are important differences between a swimming pool and the living waters of a mountain stream and the deep depths of a lake or ocean.

Living water wants to be free, free to live beyond concrete walls. And if not, we pray that justice will set it free someday, if not suddenly, then by evaporation.

Water is a metaphor for the creative transcendence and immanence of God. It begins in space as hydrogen then combining with oxygen becomes H_2O. Then it becomes atmosphere and oceans. Finally, it becomes theistic evolution in all life forms.

Water comes to earth in rain, flows into rivers, then back to oceans, seas, or is stored in ice or aquifers, or evaporates into humidity and clouds.

Water Wants to Go Home Again

In the beginning, water was free,
A gift to nature, a gift to me,
For forest, meadow, and apple trees,
For insect, animal, and life in sea,

Veiled in rainbow, fog and mist,
Singing in brooks and waterfalls,
Wild in miles of hurricanes,
Frozen in arctic snow and ice.

Awake in wells, no window light,
Dreaming in ancient aquifers,
Sand, gravel, and layered rock,
Uniting in ocean's essential salt.

Prisoner in toilets, sewage plants,
Enslaved in slime, oil and grease,
Poisoned in chemical factory waste,
Married to mercury and to lead,

Scrambling genes, deadening brains.
Water cries in human tears,
Water wants to go home again,
Be just H_2O again.

Written in 2014.

Good Medicine

Nature heals: I suppose that truth can be stated in other words by theology and contemporary psychology, but the end result is the same, if the remedy is successful.

For Native Americans, anything that helped them on their journey through life, kept them in harmony with the Great Spirit, healed their minds and bodies, and helped them find their rightful place in the scheme of things was good medicine. Once more, that which gave them strength and wisdom and made spirit and body healthy was good medicine. They also knew that constant association with troubled and difficult people tended to confuse and weaken them. The remedy was solitude in wilderness.

Good medicine was drinking spring water flowing between slabs of limestone—mineral medicine. Handfuls of this water lifted to lips made them one with the earth and sky.

Good medicine was teaching my grandson and his friend the art of fly fishing and showing them how to catch wily German Brown trout with a Peacock Lady fly. If one only needs lots of big fish, a supermarket will do, but if one wants the good medicine of the mountain stream, a couple of firm fish for lunch was enough.

Good medicine was sharing the forest with a black bear. When this hungry bear smelled our bacon and egg breakfast on our pickup's tailgate, it came running. Puzzled, we heard it thrashing through the thick underbrush for a couple of minutes before it came into view. Whew! We were ready to give that bear our breakfast, but when the bear saw us, it stopped short, turned around and ran the other away. This bear's mother taught it well to be afraid of humans. The boys stayed close to me after that. This bear was good medicine.

We saw a wild turkey hen and her juvenile brood, and enough deer to fill a copy of *Field and Stream*.

Good medicine was ponderosa pine, blue spruce, and quaking aspen towering above wild berries and forest ferns. Unspoiled air, thin and clean, breathed to the bottom of lungs, was good medicine. Damp forest mulch full of the spice of life and soft to the touch was good medicine for bare feet.

We went to the White Mountains on the Apache Indian Reservation in Arizona to fish and find solitude among the pines and to drink again from Diamond Creek. We found much more. We found good medicine.

Written in 2000.

Roosevelt Lake

Roosevelt Lake is a large reservoir formed by a dam on the Salt River in Arizona. Roosevelt hugs the sides of its deep canyon basin, wicking moisture to thirsty desert flora.

Bob Simbric, Phil England, and I were going to visit Roosevelt Lake, north of Phoenix, for a day of relaxed fishing.

Moving down the Beeline Highway we stopped at Pumpkin Center for breakfast, and then drove through the pristine desert landscape. In the rising sun, mountains were pink with highlights and lavender in shadows. Here is the slow awakening of life to another day. Our mood is relaxed and free. It's now cool, but when the sun is full strength overhead, gun metal will be too hot to touch and a sunburn will be minutes away from bare skin.

This lake seems out of place in this high desert, too much water, too wet. Now, a cooling breeze energizes boaters, but later hot and sullen heat will drive most to shade and shore.

Fast boats pull skiers like puppets on a string and their waves rock our boat.

Vegetation near the water is rich-green and prosperous like rich folks in beachfront condos, while cacti and greasewood up the slopes struggle in dry poverty.

In the shadows of first light, desert birds call one to another and, if I am quiet and still, I will see quail coming to water. They will be thirsty after feeding on dry seeds. Cautiously, they will come to Roosevelt water.

Mesquite and catclaw thickets are in bloom with butter colored catkins, sweet and heavy with nectar. Being a beekeeper I notice such things. I felt a sudden urge to place bee hives among this sweetness, but it quickly passed, too far to tend.

Silent and lonely saguaro cacti frame the mountains with uplifted arms as if praying for water or directing a hallelujah chorus. Their prayers will work; rains will come in time, and all will be well again. There is comfort in knowing this

Then again, if I listened to my inner voice, I hear the parched land cry in thirst, and if I have the imagination to see such things, I will see a solitary prospector and his burro searching for a lost gold mine by a map he bought in a bar in Florence Junction.

Early morning between four and nine is the best time to fish Roosevelt Lake. After that, the sun bakes the hills and flat-irons the lake. Tormented by thirst, Apache cattle come and stand belly deep in the cooling water. Fishermen either retreat to shade or hide under boat umbrellas. Fish swim deep.

This high desert's stillness and peace is in sharp contrast to the noisy business in my other world. This is paradise as close as we will get this side of Eden. Words fail. A prodigal from Eden, I questioned my right to be here in such beauty and wonder. Each time I visit this Eden place it's always the first time. Visits change me. I can't go back to who I was.

This is what it means for me to visit this lake again; to be with friends again. And as an artist and poet, I saw once more this natural beauty in a new way, and discover my latent innocence again.

And so it was, after this holiday, we must go back to the world of Man. We ate and freely talked as friends do. The sun rose and set. We watched the day unfold and drift again to sleep. But we will come again someday, together or I alone, to get our soul's laundry done, and then be on our pilgrim's way.

Some day

Someday I will lay,
This mortal body,
Of dust and clay,
In the ground,
In gratitude.

Some day I will have,
A body light and water,
A rainbowed body,
Arching from Earth,
To stars.

Written in 2000.

Acknowledgements

I am thankful for the encouragement of my wife Doris and our family and friends in writing and publishing this book.

In gratitude, I acknowledge librarian Amber Polo's leadership and teaching in the Camp Verde Community Library, particularly her publishing guidance.

Furthermore, I am indebted to all those patient and long-suffering people who helped shape my life, especially my parents, hopeful teachers, professors, military personnel, church leaders and congregations. They had faith in me when I showed little promise. They instilled high ideals, a thirst for knowledge, and imparted their gifts of experience and wisdom. They also challenged me to work hard and succeed.

Once more, I owe my gratitude to Yavapai College teachers and authors who taught creative writing courses and encouraged me to apply myself in the discipline of writing readable stories.

Finally, I am thankful for God's love and Grace in my life.

Free

★ *The weekend edition* ★

Free

Verde View

Serving the Verde Valley and the Red Rock country of Arizona

Volume 9, Number 31

Friday, August 10, 1979

About the Author

John Jenkins was born March 21, 1930 in Kalamazoo, Michigan. He briefly lived in Battle Creek, and then on a farm in Fulton, Michigan for the duration of World War II. In 1947, he served an enlistment in the Air Force and trained as an aircraft mechanic. He was stationed on Okinawa and studied in Japan.

John earned a B.A. degree, majoring in Bible with a minor in education at Linda Vista Baptist Bible College and Seminary in 1958. He completed a creative writing course at Yavapai College, Verde Valley Campus, and wrote "A Voice in the Wilderness," a column in the *Verde View* and *The Journal* newspapers in Camp Verde, Arizona in the 1970s and 80s.

In preparation for pastoral ministry, John and Doris served two churches in the San Diego area and as a pastoral family served five churches in Arizona: Duncan, Winslow, Camp Verde, and Patagonia Community Church, with an interim ministry at the Camp Verde United Methodist Church.

John served as chairman of the Chaplaincy Program at the Marcus Lawrence Hospital, now Verde Valley Medical

Center in Cottonwood, Arizona. He was a board member of the Verde Valley Guidance Clinic. Furthermore, John served as scoutmaster in three pastoral communities and was the recipient of the Silver Beaver Award.

He served as a volunteer fireman in Duncan, Arizona, and an ambulance driver in two pastoral communities. He was awarded the Verde Valley Chamber of Commerce "1974 Man of the Year Award," which he shared with Doris. Along with his church ministry in Camp Verde he served as a substitute teacher and school bus driver. He served on the original Camp Verde Community Library building committee, now the new Library's parking lot.

John hiked the Grand Canyon many times with several groups, including his Scout Troops. He also hiked several times with others into the Havasupai Canyon.

John and Doris bicycled in Linda Vista. John is a gardener and beekeeper. He tended exponentially up to 70-90 hives for twenty years. John is also an artist, poet, writer, and fly fisherman, as well as the author of *A Voice in the Wilderness*, a book of inspirational essays.

In the summer of 1985, John bicycled from Florence, Oregon to Yorktown, Virginia by way of the TransAmerica Bicycle Trail while Doris drove their camper as backup. With historical sidebars and inspirational insights, John wrote *Catching A Dream: A Bicycle Journey Across America*, a day-by-day journal of their sacred journey in the slow lane, coast to coast across America.

In 1986, John bicycled "The Grand Canyon to Mexico Almost Across Arizona Bicycle Tour," and in November 1988, rode the Third Annual "MS Best Dam Bike Get-Together in the Southwest" from Phoenix to Parker Dam on the Colorado River. Doris was his backup.

John and Doris lived in Arizona since 1958 and in the Verde Valley since 1965. After sixty-years of marriage, Doris passed on to her reward, March 21 on John's birthday, 2011. She is continually missed. John and Doris have three children, seven grandchildren, and eleven great-grandchildren.

Currently, John is a volunteer chaplain at the Verde Valley Medical Center. Creative writing and photography remain high on John's list of interests.

John lives in Camp Verde and daily visits the new Camp Verde Community Library and walks about town meeting friends and strangers who often become friends. John is 88 years old and active in church and community.